Old Bristle Almanac

Harry Stoke & Vinny Green

**This book is dedicated to
Georgina, Charlie, Erin, Louis
and Sarah, Victoria, Sam, Megan**

*Thanks for being as patient
and understanding as ever*

Published by Broadcast Books
7 Exeter Buildings
Redland
Bristol BS6 6TH
Tel: 0117 9238891

www.bristolpublishers.co.uk
catherine@broadcastbooks.co.uk

Cover design: Ira Rainey

Cover image: © Photographer: Cora Reed | Agency: Dreamstime.com

Printed in Great Britain by Cromwell Press Ltd, Trowbridge, Wilts

Special thanks go to
Eugene Byrne at *Venue*, and
Chris Kelly at *BBC Bristol*
for unswervingly supporting
everything we have ever done.

INTRODUCTION

Welcome to the *Old Bristle Almanac*. But what is an almanac all about, I hear you ask? Well I guess that depends on who you ask. Historically, an almanac would be a book of calendar-based tables giving you astrological information. This would help you know when to plant your crops, when the moon was at its lowest, or when the high tides might be. Quite useful if you were a medieval farmer who lived by the sea and could actually read.

More recent almanacs are collections of facts, statistics, and miscellany about a particular subject for a given time period, such as sporting results, for example. This would of course be useful if you invented a time machine and went back in time with the aim of using such information to make pots of money, as demonstrated by Biff Tannen in *Back to the Future Part II*.

So taking both formats under our wings we have created a hybrid: a unique collection of Bristol-related information, past, present, and future. So if you feel that you need help and guidance to get through the maze that is the city centre of life, then we can do that with Rose Green's horoscopes, predictions, and advice from beyond the grave, with guest appearances by Isambard Kingdom Brunel.

Alternatively, if you are the kind of person who only ventures out of the house for the odd pub quiz (and even then only because they give out free crisps) then this book is a wealth of Bristol knowledge and facts that might prove invaluable in your quest, especially if the quizmaster decides to take his questions from it.

With such a wide spectrum of skills required to put together a book like this we have enlisted the powers of Bristol's very own psychic, Rose Green. Cross her palm with a packet of Happy Shopper Rich Tea biscuits and there's nothing she can't do.

Rose is a relic of a passing age; an era when every third household had some old Doris who could read your fortune from your tea leaves. Partly perhaps because, after the war, people wanted to believe the future really could be bright and rosy. That and partly because nobody had a telly – oh yes, you made your own entertainment in those days.

Education and advances in science (particularly the science of teabags) brought an end to widespread acceptance of that sort of thing. It's a shame really, but ultimately just another sign of changing times. Luckily for us, Rose is multi-skilled and can read not just tea leaves, but also the Bristolian night sky and the *Western Daily Press*.

So between the covers of this book lies your guide for the coming year. Brace yourself, it's going to be a bumpy ride, but a fun one to boot. So enjoy it – you'll only live it once.

Harry Stoke
Bristol, UK

JANUARY

No news is good news
(at least it works for the Bristol Observer)

As a year of celebrations get under way in Liverpool to commemorate winning the title of *2008 City of Culture*, an inquest will be launched into exactly how a city that gave us Ken Dodd, Cilla Black, and Stan Boardman could possibly be considered more cultured than Bristol.

Around the start of the month hundreds of people will queue overnight outside Debenhams in Broadmead in sub-zero temperatures in a bid to secure last season's cut-price beachwear, flip-flops, and a paddling pool. The sales will, however, start late as the rest of the queue fail to realise the bearded man at the front actually sleeps in the doorway every night.

Bristol City Council will announce another year of Isambard Kingdom Brunel-related celebrations, this time to commemorate the 150th anniversary of the year before he died. Events will include a tallest hat competition, an exhibition of Brunel's favourite hats, and a series of cookery workshops themed around French hat-based cuisine.

A naked man will this month be left dangling from the Clifton Suspension Bridge after a New Year's bet goes horribly wrong. After agreeing to bungee jump from the bridge using only his friends' underpants as a safety cord, problems will arise when only three of his friends agree to remove their underwear, leaving the stuntman suspended by just two pairs of boxer shorts and a thong.

HOROSCOPES *by Rose Green*

 ## Aquarius *(Jan 21 - Feb 19)*

With the New Year comes a time for reflection and perhaps a change of direction in your career. Being short tempered, unreliable, unreasonable, argumentative and bad tempered may not seem attractive to most employers, but Bristol will always need more bus drivers.

 ## Pisces *(Feb 20 - Mar 20)*

After spending a solitary and miserable Christmas you should accept the need to get out and broaden your horizons. Now is the time to meet new people in exciting locations. Learn their customs and ways of life and soak up the local atmosphere. They may dress in a strange way and do a silly dance to greet you, but that's just Clevedon for you.

 ## Aries *(Mar 21 - Apr 20)*

The Lucky House Takeaway in Westbury on Trym or The Lucky House Fish & Chip Shop in Ashton, the choice is yours. Neither will be lucky for you this month but they both do a nice Clark's pie. The Lucky Dragon Chinese restaurant in Hambrook, however, is very lucky if you happen to be a dragon.

Taurus *(Apr 21 - May 21)*

What a start to the year. You decided to exchange that jumper your aunt bought you for Christmas, then spent six hours in a traffic jam trying to get into The Mall. What happened when you finally get to John Lewis? The shop assistant threatens to gouge your eyes out with a spoon. Perhaps the jumper isn't so bad after all.

Gemini *(May 22 - Jun 21)*

It's time for you to plan the family holiday. Forget the brochures showing far-off destinations with golden beaches. Instead, pack the family off to Weston-super-Mare. Not only will the holiday cost less, but also one dip in the sea and the lights in your house will work without you turning them on.

Cancer *(Jun 22 - Jul 23)*

Honesty is a virtue. It's what we look for in friends and work colleagues. Sometimes the hardest person in the world to be honest with is yourself. So now, repeat after me: I live in Southmead, not Westbury on Trym. I live in Southmead, not Westbury on Trym.

HOROSCOPES *by Rose Green*

 Leo *(Jul 24 - Aug 23)*

You are in a circle of despair. Try to spend this month thinking of the positives in your life, however small they may be. So you have lost your job, your family, you are up to your eyeballs in debt and you still have to fund a £500 a day drug habit. Where's the positive? Well, the Festival of the Sea may be returning to Bristol in 2008.

 Virgo *(Aug 24 - Sep 23)*

Health issues become a worry later this month after a slight tumble gets you a couple of weeks stay in the BRI. But don't worry about it too much. It's not that the injury will be that serious, it's just that it'll take that long for somebody to see you in A&E.

 Libra *(Sep 24 - Oct 23)*

Financial matters feature very favourably for you this month. In fact, so favourably, you are definitely going to win the lottery. Tell your boss to stick his job today in preparation for your big windfall, and then sign contracts on the biggest Clifton townhouse on the market. PS: I've been drinking.

 ## Scorpio *(Oct 24 - Nov 22)*

Think before you act this month as the alignment of the stars could so easily guide you into doing things that you may never normally consider and you could end up looking a tad silly. Accepting a change ticket on a bus, ok; wearing white socks with jeans, dodgy; playing Frisbee on the downs, complete idiot.

 ## Sagittarius *(Nov 23 - Dec 21)*

After spending so much time living on your own, love will finally come knocking on your Staple Hill door this month. Unfortunately, I cannot specify whether it will be AM or PM. Better wait in all day than let love pass you by.

 ## Capricorn *(Dec 22 - Jan 20)*

Now is the ideal time for you to launch that new business you've been thinking about for so long. The moon's low position over Dundry Hill this month means there has never been a better time to open an expensive Mediterranean deli on Filwood Broadway. It simply cannot fail.

Cary Grant

b. Jan 18th 1904 – d. Nov 29th 1986

Born Archibald Alexander Leach, Academy Award winning Grant is arguably the greatest British actor ever to come out of Horfield (not the prison). A product of the golden age of cinema, when men were men and real life was still in black and white, Grant's image was perpetually suave, cool, and quick-witted; certainly more debonair than Debenhams.

His interest in theatre was sparked from a backstage visit to the Bristol Hippodrome as a child, but life was not always rosy for Grant. While he was at school one day, his father committed his mother to a mental institution (something he would not discover for twenty years). He ran away with a travelling stage group, only to be sent home once they discovered he was only thirteen.

After being expelled from school, he rejoined the group and in 1920 followed in Cabot's wake and set sail for America. After splitting from the troupe when they returned to Britain, he stayed briefly in New York before moving to Hollywood in 1931. It was there he signed a contract with Paramount and changed his name. The rest, as film historians would say, is history.

Despite his movie stardom, Grant remained a regular visitor to Bristol. Many commentators put this down to the lack of decent cider in Tinsel town, but it could also have been because his old mum still lived here. It seemed natural to commemorate such a Bristol legend with a statue in the city, so to honour his achievements, in 2001 a life-sized statue of Grant was erected outside Bristol's well-known theatrical establishment, Lloyds TSB.

Bristol's First Boy Racer

Schoolteacher George Pocock was one of Bristol's great eccentric inventors. When Brunel was still digging holes through rocks, Pocock invented a caning machine to give schoolboys a walloping they'd remember, all without giving him an arm-ache. But thrashing kids didn't fill his time (not once he'd invented a machine to do it for him), and when he wasn't playing the organ, or preaching to peasants in Kingswood, he liked playing with kites. Big ones.

Not content with mucking about on the Downs on a Sunday afternoon, Pocock dreamt that wind-power could transport people. His daughter Martha (who later in life would give birth to the bearded marvel WG Grace) became the first 'volunteer' to test his idea when she was hoisted 270 feet into the air over the Avon Gorge strapped to a chair.

In 1826, Pocock evolved the idea and patented a kite-drawn carriage, called the Char Volant. Pulled by two kites, the vehicle was capable of carrying up to six people over vast distances and reaching considerable speeds (as long as it was windy of course). On January 8th 1827, whilst travelling from Bristol to London, it was recorded at a speed of almost 20mph – not fast today, but in 1827 that was greased lightning. He was Bristol's first boy racer.

Alas, like a pre-runner to the Sinclair C5, Pocock's Char Volant failed to revolutionise the world of transport. Despite being cheap and environmentally friendly (not something the Victorians cared much about), poor steering, nice weather, and the eventual introduction of overhead power cables saw any hope of this being the future disappear forever.

January

World Wedding Fayres

Anyone planning a wedding is well catered for this month with not one, but two wedding fayres taking place in Bristol – one at the luxurious Holiday Inn Filton (honeymoon packages available), and one at the Bristol Marriott Hotel Broadmead.

Weddings can be an expensive occasion, and a visit to either exhibition will certainly back that up. Advertised as a one-stop wedding shop, exhibitors from all around the region will be on hand to offer advice, prices, and flyers. In fact, the only thing you will be unable to buy at the event is the partner (but there's always the internet for that).

Every kind of wedding is catered for here, from the large to the small, from the wacky to the wonderful, although probably not the inexpensive. It doesn't even matter if you are the only gay at the exhibition as civil partnerships are also covered. With over ninety stalls and a fashion show, it's a full day. On the event website, singer Dave Dean describes it as "a great day, the best fun I've had in ages", although we're unsure how often he gets out.

If nothing else, you can put an end to the sleepless nights worrying about your uncle filming the wedding using an 8mm cine camera or your brother trying to drive you to the church in a stolen Datsun Cherry. Instead you can replace them with sleepless nights worrying about how you are going to pay for all the stuff you get convinced you need. But keep smiling, because hey – it's going to be the happiest day of your life.

Dear IKB

I need some advice on my marriage. Things just seem to be going from bad to worse. We used to be happy in each other's company, but now all we seem to do is argue. Do you think sleeping with her sister has soured the relationship?

Anon

IKB SAYS:

The success of my marriage was based on love, trust and the fact that I never saw her. To be honest, I was too busy working to be bothered with petty arguments or sleeping with in-laws.

What you need to do to ensure your old chap stays in your trousers is hard work, and lots of it. Nowadays if someone stays in work past 4 o'clock, it's considered to be working late. In my day you worked for 18 hours and slept the other six. You had no time for minor distractions like talking to your wife or knobbing her sister.

Hard work – that was the key to my success, and early death. Also I never went in for all this jealousy business: 'are you looking at my wife'? I don't care; I'm not there. Mind you, if you criticised my 7-foot Broad Gauge Railway design, I would have had to ask you to step outside.

MISCELLANY

Tide Times

Floating Harbour – Always in
Weston-super-Mare – Always out
River Avon – In and out
Eastville Park Boating Lake – Shake it all about

2008 Anniversaries

WG Grace born *(160 years)*
Bristol Rugby Club founded *(120 years)*
Speedway starts at Knowle *(80 years)*
The Great Bristol Flood *(40 years)*
First trunk telephone call made by the Queen *(50 years)*
Industrial Museum opened *(30 years)*

Things Bristol Will Probably Never See

Decent public transport
A reduction in council tax
Congestion-free roads
An arena
Premiership football

FEBRUARY

Beauty is only skin deep
(even if she is a munter)

PREDICTIONS *by Rose Green*

After the new edition of *The Big Fundraiser Invitation Book* is launched this month, fashionable restaurant *Severnshed* will be swamped with cardholders after the book misprints the discount they are offering as 500% instead of 50%. The thought of having to give money back to card-holding diners forces the restaurant to close its doors until all editions of the book are recalled.

A new plan will be proposed to extend the main runway at Bristol International Airport. The scheme, which it is hoped will be in place for the summer rush, will go further than previous plans to just edge a bit over the A38, by taking the runway the full seventy-five miles to Exeter. Seeing as it's where most flights end up when they can't land at Lulsgate anyway, it seems a natural choice.

Bristol City Council will unveil a controversial new plan this month to clear the notorious Bear Pit in Broadmead of beggars – by sealing it off and filling it with real bears. Reminiscent of scenes of ancient Rome, the troubled underpass will become a gladiatorial pit for a week with the surrounding roads closed for spectators.

As property prices in Bristol continue to rise, creating a shortage of affordable housing, the control room on the Plimsoll Swing Bridge will be marketed as a 'compact luxury studio flat' offering 'extensive views over the harbourside'. However, prospective buyers of the twelve by eight foot apartment could be put off once they discover the bridge will still be swinging (not at parties).

February

Aquarius *(Jan 21 - Feb 19)*

It's the time for romance again. Valentine's Day, a perfect time to make a full-blown gesture to show them how much you love them. You thought about a weekend in a top hotel, or maybe a slap-up meal in a fancy restaurant, but eventually have decided to buy her a card from Clinton Cards in Broadmead. Blimey, are you really thinking of spending that sort of money?

Pisces *(Feb 20 - Mar 20)*

Unlucky in love? Maybe it's because you're about as attractive as a pound of tripe in a butcher's shop window. Never mind, whatever your appearance, why not try the latest craze: speed dating. Get your fat ass up to Channings on a Thursday night and somebody will talk to you, even if it is only for three minutes.

Aries *(Mar 21 - Apr 20)*

You have been depressed recently. After all the partying you did in December, January was always going to be a really quiet month. Never mind, you've still got February to rediscover the party animal in you. And just look at what you've got to look forward to: Valentines Day, Pancake Day, um... All right, it's going to be another shit month.

HOROSCOPES *by Rose Green*

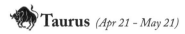 **Taurus** *(Apr 21 - May 21)*

Lost touch with old acquaintances that have moved away from the Bristol area? Perhaps it's time to pop into one of the Internet cafes on Baldwin Street and send them an email. Arranging a meeting is the only way to realise why you have lost touch with the big-headed loud mouths in the first place.

 Gemini *(May 22 - Jun 21)*

With so many young students swarming around the harbourside bars in the evenings, you might be starting to feel old. The bad news is if you think you are, then you probably are. Sure, go to the nightclub anyway and stand at the bar, but you'll only look like somebody's parent waiting to take them home. Life sucks.

 Cancer *(Jun 22 - Jul 23)*

Leaving Temple Meads, cross the Railway Bridge and then bear right at the Three Lamps junction and carry straight on up the hill. Bear right at the next set of traffic lights and then take the 2nd right. Arrive at your destination.

HOROSCOPES *by Rose Green*

February

 ## Leo *(Jul 24 - Aug 23)*

Now is the time to break out and try and discover the real you. Beware though, a journey taken with a Cancerian may not be, as first thought, one of fulfilment and discovery, but instead a trip to Totterdown.

 ## Virgo *(Aug 24 - Sep 23)*

You may still be feeling the effects from the powerful moon of Saturn; or could it be the kebab you purchased on Park Street last night? Either way, travel is probably not an option for the remainder of this month unless the coach has a toilet or you're wearing brown trousers.

 ## Libra *(Sep 24 - Oct 23)*

You are very naïve when it comes to intimate relationships. When an attractive young woman you have fancied for ages tells you she wants to make beautiful music together, you end up in a panic because you can't play an instrument. The instrument she was referring to is not musical – if you're not sure, pop into Ann Summers in Broadmead and buy a video.

HOROSCOPES *by Rose Green*

 Scorpio *(Oct 24 - Nov 22)*

It really is no good allowing things to get on top of you so much that you're sat with your head in your hands crying. Firstly, it doesn't solve anything, and secondly your bus-load of passengers are going to get pretty pissed off if you don't get that 75 up Gloucester Road pretty soon.

 Sagittarius *(Nov 23 - Dec 21)*

Waiting for the perfect partner to come along can be like waiting for the 75 up the Gloucester Road – you are living more in hope than expectation. Maybe you are setting the bar too high; forget Brad Pitt, Tom Cruise or Russell Crowe. Think more Richard Angwin, Bob Crampton or Clinton Rogers. Real men, not movie stars.

 Capricorn *(Dec 22 - Jan 20)*

There's nothing like Valentine's Day to make you admit to yourself that your social life needs a kick up the ass. It's never nice facing up to reality, but talking to a woman over a drink until the early hours is really not the same as buying a bottle of shandy at Asda in Bedminster at three in the morning.

Lee Evans

b. Feb 25th 1964

Probably best known as a sweaty stand-up comedian who gets through suits like a curry fan gets through toilet roll, his hyperactive physical style of comedy has led some to suggest he must be on some form of chemical substance. On them? He's full of them. After growing up in Avonmouth, it's hard not to be.

Following a big break at the Edinburgh Festival in 1988 (career not bones), he went on to win the prestigious Perrier Comedy award in 1993 for his energetic slapstick, work he previously described as 'complete pap'. He has since made the tricky transition from stand-up comedian to successful actor that very few have managed (just ask Eddie Izzard). His appearances in smash-hit movies such as *Mousehunt, Funny Bones* and *Something About Mary* turned him into an international star and has led to him working with many of Hollywood's A-list celebrities, as well as Brenda Blethyn.

Not wanting to turn his back on stand-up completely, Evans has continued to tour and in 2005 he entered the *Guinness Book of Records* for a 'solo act performing to the biggest comedy audience' when he performed in front of 10,108 people in Manchester.

Pap or not he can still fill Wembley Arena or sell a shed load of DVDs at the drop of a hat, something most comedians could only dream of, as are the six-figure advertising contracts he constantly turns down. A funny bloke and a nice one to boot – even if he is from Avonmouth.

Gold, always believe in your soul...

Whereas today the only ice skating most people watch on television involves D-list celebrities generally making fools of themselves in the vain hope of getting a presenting job on QVC, the 1970s and early 1980s were the heyday of British figure skating and Bristolian Robin Cousins was at the heart of it.

On February 21st 1980, millions tuned in their TV sets to watch Cousins triple jump and double axel his little heart out, taking the gold medal for men's figure skating at the Winter Olympics. It was a truly awesome performance (look it up on *YouTube*), but sadly Britain's only medal of the Games. Where's a girl on a tea tray when you need her?

Cousins started skating at age nine, quickly proving to be a natural. While most visitors to the Mecca Ice Rink were content with kissing behind the DJ booth or trying to get served in the bar, Cousins actually went there to skate. By age 12, he had won a national skating title, and at 14 he was junior champion. He then went on to represent Great Britain and win a host of titles, culminating in his Olympic Gold.

Cousins was also awarded an MBE for services to sport and skating, and was made *BBC Sports Personality of the Year* in 1980. His ultimate accolade though undoubtedly came when Bristol City Council named a sports centre in Avonmouth after him, allowing future generations of Bristolians to follow in his icy grooves – except, of course, it didn't have an ice rink.

February

Potty 1 - Bullies 0

Singing sensation Paul Potts took the country by storm when he won the first series of *Britain's Got Talent*, netting himself £100,000 in prize money, a place on the *Royal Variety Performance*, and a major recording deal with Mr High Waisters himself, Simon Cowell.

Potts was born and raised in Fishponds and attended Chester Park Primary, before later going on to study at St Mary Redcliffe School. But far from being his best years, this was not a happy period in his life, what with having to contend with constant playground bullying and the fact he lived in Fishponds.

After leaving school, Paul got a job as a shelf stacker at Tesco in Eastville. While working in the freezer section he would often impress his colleagues with his singing, although these impromptu concerts would frequently be interrupted by people wanting to know the whereabouts of the Findus Crispy Pancakes.

After quitting pancakes for politics, he went on to become a Liberal Democrat Councillor on Bristol City Council representing Eastville. However after several years in the role, he finally stood down in 2003 to get a proper job at Carphone Warehouse.

Described as a shy and humble man – a few years in show business could change that – Paul's triumphant return to Bristol will certainly be one in the eye for all those meathead bullies who made his life hell at school. Who's the loser now?

Dear IKB

As an engineer of great standing, you are my last hope of ever finding happiness. Could you give me some advice on finding a partner? I am five foot tall, single, live with my mum, and I have never found a woman who shares my interests: namely stamp collecting, model railways, and cataloguing my large collection of cheese labels. Can you help?

Jeremy, Bradley Stoke

IKB SAYS:

The first thing you need to understand is a man should be a man – women will respect you for it. None of this: "I'll cook tea tonight", "Shall I put the Hoover round?" or "Can I wear your knickers?" No, you should make it clear that your job is the breadwinner, so do not even attempt to partner up with somebody who has a job or smokes a cigar.

Women also like a man of stature – what I lacked in height, I more than made up for in hat. So as you too are short, only concentrate on meeting women shorter than yourself. If this is not possible, invest in some platform shoes.

Many a woman spent a perfectly adequate evening underground watching me dig. But I have yet to meet a woman who wasn't impressed with the line, "Shall I show you my width?" For some reason they seemed disappointed when they realised I was talking about my broad gauge railway. At the end of the day, you need to be with somebody who accepts you for who you are: a stamp-collecting, train and cheese-loving pigmy freak.

February

♥ •♥ MISCELLANY ♥• ♥

This Valentine's Day, forget the expensive dinner, the clichéd roses, and the industrial size tub of chocolate body paint (with roller) and woo your partner with some simple Bristolian poetry.

> If I done a drawlen of ee
> It'd be of a gurt big art
> Cause every time yoom catch my eye
> I still fink yoom proper smart

> I ain't very ansum
> I ain't very tall
> But gif I anudder chance
> I'll take thee down Ikeawl

> Me luv fer you is gurt macky
> Me luv fer you is gurt lush
> If you play yer cards right me babber
> I let thee share me tuffbrush

> Your eyes are like a lush choclut
> Your skin's soft as pitchen snow
> Not that I really noticed
> But ar muh told I so

Ee luvs I
An I luvs ee
We don't need lots a words
To say weem appy

I may not have style
I may not have class
But say you'll be me Valentine
An I'll take thee up the Gas!

I finks yoom gurt lush
Where's bin all me life?
Now that I found you
Ullee be me wife?

Your ead is evsa prittee
What more can I say?
Yoom as tasty as a cawd Blakforn
On a luverly summer's day

MARCH

The shortest journey starts with a long wait for a bus

PREDICTIONS

by Rose Green

A group of Czech men visiting the city for a stag weekend will spend the night trying to find a specialist lap-dancing club they found on a city tourism map: the Temple Circus Gyratory. The unfortunate mix-up will come to light when police find the six exhausted men in the early hours of the morning asleep on a roundabout at the Temple Meads end of Temple Way.

March

City Council leaders in Bristol will issue a stark warning this month that council tax in the city may need to rise to help pay for the recent rise in council tax. Council auditors will discover that the administrative cost of the annual council tax increase will this year be higher than predicted, so to cover this, the tax will need to rise once again.

A tow-truck working on behalf of Bristol City Council will itself be towed away after being caught parking illegally whilst hooking up a car that was parked on double yellow lines. The driver of the impounded lorry will face fines of several hundred pounds, twice the standard tow-away and penalty charges, as the two vehicles were already connected when the truck is hooked up.

No league tables will be needed this month to highlight falling education standards in the area after a Bristol youth becomes injured whilst attempting the latest craze, Tomb Stoning. Coastguards warn that jumping into water from a great height will always be fraught with danger, but jumping from Weston Pier when the tide is out is just plain stupid.

HOROSCOPES *by Rose Green*

Aquarius *(Jan 21 - Feb 19)*

What a dilemma St Patrick's Day throws up. If you had some Irish descendants you would have a real excuse to celebrate it. Trouble is, all your family are from Bristol and the furthest they have ever moved is Pensford. But just think for a minute – didn't your Uncle once have an Irish Setter? Line up the Guinness and top of the morning to you!

Pisces *(Feb 20 - Mar 20)*

Your energy levels will continue to stay high for the early part of this month, so why not make the most of it. Why don't you get down the gym and start training early for the Bristol Half Marathon? Who said that drinking two hundred cans of Red Bull for Sport Relief would come to no good?

Aries *(Mar 21 - Apr 20)*

A family funeral is always a tense occasion. Emotions are raw and people end up doing and saying things they don't mean. One relative punched you; another tried to strangle you, while the rest just called you sick. Who would have thought that a bunch of inflatable flowers could cause so much family conflict? On the plus side, they certainly stood out at the crematorium.

March

Taurus *(Apr 21 - May 21)*

You know how important your mum is to you. She is always there for you – if she isn't in the pub. So let's not repeat last year's disaster on Mothering Sunday. Take her for a meal at a top Bristol restaurant; treat her to some jewellery, some perfume or some new clothes. Anything will do, but please, no more inflatable flowers from Poundstretchers.

Gemini *(May 22 - Jun 21)*

You have always followed the rule 'you have to speculate to accumulate'. So after spending thousands of pounds phoning competitions on *Richard and Judy*, *GMTV* and *Blue Peter*, you discover the calls never even got registered and you might as well have flushed your money down the toilet. I bet even Bob Crampton never gave away one of his weather umbrellas, the bastard.

Cancer *(Jun 22 - Jul 23)*

You have waited so long for this moment and now it's almost here. Going to work in the dark, coming home in the dark, freezing cold weather, it will soon be behind you. That's right, British summer is about to begin. But before you put away your jumpers, pop on your shorts, and head straight for College Green, just remember – it's still only March.

March

 Leo *(Jul 24 - Aug 23)*

Modern life is making you paranoid and out of pocket. Just the other day you thought you were the victim of identity theft when you discovered someone rifling through your bins. It turned out to be a tramp chasing the remains of a chicken dinner, but you had already rushed out to buy a £100 paper shredder. At least you can take it back. What? You've already shredded the receipt?

 Virgo *(Aug 24 - Sep 23)*

You've been busy lately, so give yourself some time off. Sit back for a few hours and do nothing. Relax, read the paper, stare out of the window, even have a snooze. It might seem a bit irresponsible at first, but there's not a lot else to do when you're stuck in traffic on the M32.

 Libra *(Sep 24 - Oct 23)*

As if St Patrick's Day didn't cause you enough trouble, now you have to worry about St David's day as well. If only you had some Welsh descendants you'd go out and celebrate it. Then again, that would probably involve some form of wearing daffodils and singing in an all-male choir. So at the end of the day, who gives a toss if anyone in your family is Welsh?

March

Scorpio *(Oct 24 - Nov 22)*

Life is never easy when you discover your own child is afflicted with a disability. As a parent you always aim to give them as normal a life as possible, hoping that, as an adult, they will find a role in an accepting society. Well, if colour-blindness is the affliction, you're in luck – First Bus are always hiring. What red light?

Sagittarius *(Nov 23 - Dec 21)*

This month you should treat a loved one to a romantic night out on the town. That doesn't mean an evening spent drinking Natch in the Barley Mow followed by a Miss Millies Mega Bucket and a good old-fashioned punch up on the way home. What sort of woman are you?

Capricorn *(Dec 22 - Jan 20)*

Why not let your natural caring side come to the forefront this month. I am sure many of the people you work with will enjoy you mothering them. Be warned though, while being a shoulder to cry on and a person to turn to for advice is fine, spitting on your hanky and rubbing it in your boss's face at an important business meeting will probably not be appreciated.

Ian Holloway

b. Mar 12th 1963

March

When the BBC's *Football Focus* programme asked supporters from around the country to vote for their club's all time 'Cult Heroes', it was no surprise when Ian Holloway received 75% of all votes cast by Bristol Rovers fans. Ian quite simply is 'Mr Bristol Rovers', though many Bristol City supporters often use a word similar to cult when describing him.

Born and raised in Cadbury Heath, Holloway is famed for his commitment, passion and fiery temper. He played for Rovers 247 times during three spells at the club, the last as player manager. Holloway's achievements included helping Rovers win the old Third Division Championship in 1990 (just pipping Bristol City to the title, making it even sweeter), as well as reaching Wembley for the first time in the club's history the same season.

Holloway is now enjoying a successful managerial career, though it's his colourful post-match interviews, with references to parakeets, Eskimos and ugly women, that have gained him a huge following amongst supporters and the media. You would never hear Alex Ferguson declare after a victory that he was "as chuffed as a badger at the beginning of the mating season".

Holloway remains one of the true characters in football today. It would be fantastic if he could achieve his ambition of managing in the top flight, though you wouldn't bet against him returning to Bristol Rovers in some capacity in the future, though the chances of that being in the top flight remain extremely slim.

Jenkin Protheroe

b. Unknown - d. Mar 31ˢᵗ 1783

Jenkin Protheroe was not a very nice man. That's probably why, in 1783, he was hanged at the Clifton gallows. Well actually it was for the murder of a pig drover named Evan Daniel, but it's pretty much the same thing. Protheroe's execution was the last to be performed at Gallows Acre Road (later re-named as Pembroke Road), ending over two hundred years of hangings at the site.

As difficult as it may be to believe now, in the days before lights, policeman or Neighbourhood Watch, the Downs at night were a dangerous place to wander around. Whereas now you might get some drunken students and a handful of doggers, back then it was full of thieves, robbers and highwaymen. Protheroe was pretty much all of the above (although there's no evidence he was a student).

But he was no dandy highwayman. Often described as a long-armed dwarf with a twisted body and a hideous face (an 18th century version of Andrew Lloyd Webber), his distinctive features alone often terrified would-be victims into giving up their money. At the same time they also made him relatively easy to pick out of an identity parade.

After his execution, Protheroe's body was dipped in tar and placed on public display as a warning to others. Unsurprisingly this caused a real stink amongst local residents. They believed that at night he was climbing down from the gallows and haunting the surrounding area. With concerns about house prices his body was subsequently taken down and buried, bringing to an end the haunting and with it the Clifton gallows.

March

Ding ding, hold tight, going down

The Clifton Rocks Railway is something of an enigma even to those Bristolians who actually know it exists. In fact it wouldn't be unfair to classify it as the 'oddball uncle who lives in Yate' of railways.

Opened on March 11th 1893, the 500 foot long hole in the Gorge originally connected the Hotwells tram terminus to Clifton. A marvel of Victorian engineering, the carriages were dragged up the steep tracks by a combination of water and the weight of the passengers in the downward carriage.

However, whilst the funicular railway initially proved very popular, the confusion of not being able to locate it on a British Rail map made catching a connecting service from Brunel's Temple Meads station problematic.

The lack of a branch line between the two resulted in the increase of taxicabs between Temple Meads and Hotwells, which transformed the previously quiet Portway into a busy road. This, in turn, placed the lower entrance to the Rocks Railway on a dangerous main road with no pavement. Within a year, waiting Clifton-bound passengers got so fed up with being clipped by passing vehicles that usage of the service declined and you could wait days for an upward carriage. Six months later, the trains were withdrawn through lack of use.

Several alternative uses were drawn up for the tunnel, the most popular being as a large water slide carrying thrill-seekers from Clifton directly into the River Avon. However, this plan was cancelled after it was discovered that the tarmac covering of the Portway hindered the sliding of people into the river.

The Sport Relief Mile

Organisers of the BBC Sport Relief Mile will be hoping for a repeat of the 2006 event, which saw thousands of people run, walk and stumble around the one-mile course, which starts and finishes in Millennium Square.

The event is open to people of all ages and abilities, from the skeletal-framed elite athletes hoping to win the race in under four minutes to the big-boned gut lords just hoping to complete it before closing time. Whatever your ability, or lack of it, you will be welcomed with open arms.

The emphasis is not on racing but just getting involved and raising tons of cash, though pride will play a part as you really wouldn't want to get out-sprinted at the finish by an old lady on a Zimmer frame – especially if your family and friends happen to be watching.

This year's race promises to attract a host of well-known celebrities from film and television, though chances of seeing the jug-eared Mr Lineker are slim, as in reality the celebrities will probably consist of someone who occasionally reads the news on *Points West* and a couple of actors from local hospital drama *Casualty*.

Whichever way you look at it, running a mile has got to be a better way of raising money than shaving your head and filling your trousers with custard. And of course, the real exercise starts once the race is over and you have to start chasing after those tight wads who have sponsored you £1 and are now more elusive than Osama Bin Laden. Good luck, you will probably need it.

March

Dear IKB

I live in Clifton, and my problem is that I have a bad non-Bristle accent, and I want to improve it. Can you offer any advice, or invent a contraption, to Brizzlificate me.

Rob, Clifton

IKB SAYS:

Well, I couldn't say that language was ever my forte, especially the native tongue of this fine city. You see being born in Portsmouth to a French father our house was often filled with the sounds of French nautical terminology, which is very close to that of the British seafarers – only with less scurvy. However, despite all of that, your creation of the word 'Brizzlificate' has impressed me so I feel I must do everything in my power to assist you.

It seems upon further thought that there is a very simple solution to your problem, and one that I have indeed a solution to. What you must do is firstly take a train, of the steam variety of course, from Clifton Down station to Temple Meads. Upon arrival here change for a train to Bedminster station (after stopping briefly to admire my creative genius).

On arrival at Bedminster - quite simply the stronghold of the Bristolian dialect - your swanky clothing and refined language skills will ensure that you stand out like a sore thumb. In fact you will most likely be referred to locally as "the twat in the cravat". Your best plan for long-term survival in this southern borough is the wholesale adoption of the native tongue and fashion styling. It could be a matter of life or death. Three months should do it.

Surviving Fortnightly Rubbish Collections

Make better use of the space in your dustbin by climbing in at regular intervals and jumping up and down. The heavier the better, so try and get the whole family to join in, although remember that toddlers may need to be held due to Health and Safety regulations. Remember to check that no small children are still in the bin before collection.

Composting is an environmentally friendly way of disposing of such items as fruit and vegetable peelings, garden waste and grass cuttings. Simply place them in a composting bin and then in three to six months you should have perfect compost that can be emptied straight into your dustbin.

Don't forget that your bin is on wheels, so on the week it's not due for collection simply attach it to your tow bar and drive it to an area of Bristol where the bins are due to be collected. Remember to check the bin for small children before driving away.

An alternative to fortnightly collections is to just throw all of your rubbish into your front garden. This can include household waste, old electrical appliances, and even various car spares. A word of caution though, this behaviour only seems acceptable in certain parts of Bristol. Throwing a futon out of a window in Clifton Village will probably be frowned upon.

APRIL

A fool and his money are soon parted
*(particularly when **Trade-It** is involved)*

Bristol commuters will be shocked to discover the overnight introduction of congestion charging. Claiming that budget constraints have delayed the introduction of electronic number plate recognition, a man in a fluorescent donkey jacket will sit outside the Galleries car park collecting £10 in cash from every vehicle with more than three wheels. Sorry, no receipts.

The world's media will descend on Bristol when a UFO is spotted circling in the sky above Asda in Bedminster. As well as twenty-four hour blanket news coverage from television broadcasters, the story will be on the front page of every newspaper across the globe, apart from the *Bristol Observer*, which will instead carry a full page advert for the Gardiner Haskins garden furniture sale.

A Bristol business faces prosecution in the first recorded case of facial discrimination over a job advert it places warning 'munters' need not bother to apply. But a woman who applies only to be refused an interview is considering legal action in what could be a landmark case. The 41-year-old mother of nine admits she is no oil painting, but claims she is a victim of facial discrimination.

A plan to clean up graffiti on the Avon Gorge by spraying it with rock-coloured paint will backfire when the workmen become confused with the type of rock involved. The team of painters contracted to carry out the work thought they were referring to Weston-super-Mare style rock and cover the picturesque Gorge with pink paint complete with white writing.

April

 Aquarius *(Jan 21 - Feb 19)*

"Never look back", that's always been your motto. Unfortunately this resulted in you reversing over your neighbour's wife. With such scant regard for human life and lack of mirror use, surely it can only be a matter of time before you're driving a taxi around the streets of Bristol.

 Pisces *(Feb 20 - Mar 20)*

Your poor financial status could bring you down this month unless you tackle it head on. Remember charity begins at home. So why not set up a bogus one. It's cheap and easy and if you go door knocking while *Casualty* is on, people will give you money just to get rid of you.

 Aries *(Mar 21 - Apr 20)*

So you are feeling rather pleased with yourself having purchased a luxury apartment on the Bristol waterfront. Views of the docks and the *SS Great Britain* – you just can't wait to invite your friends round so you can gloat. Let's see if you're still gloating in five years time when another developer decides to build 100 homes straight in front of yours.

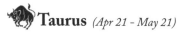 **Taurus** *(Apr 21 - May 21)*

Remember what your old dad always used to say to you? Loose lips sink ships. Well maybe during the war that was the case, but this month, as you cruise down the Feeder Canal on the *Bristol Packet*, it'll be the two-dozen lard-assed American tourists who are definitely to blame. At least you could use one of them as a raft.

Gemini *(May 22 - Jun 21)*

You've always enjoyed a bit of a laugh, and like nothing more than a good practical joke. So when you came home from work and found a note from your wife telling you she's run off with a plumber from Southmead, you thought it was hilarious. However, after three weeks the joke's starting to wear a bit thin, and just where did she hide all her clothes?

Cancer *(Jun 22 - Jul 23)*

So you want to ensure your kids get a good education. Don't bother pouring over the Bristol secondary school Ofsted results. Instead, ask yourself this simple question: can you afford to pay £4,000 a term? If the answer is no, then you can put the results away, as they are off to that failing comprehensive school just up the road.

April

Leo *(Jul 24 - Aug 23)*

You are at risk of a breakdown or totally losing control, so you really should attempt to slow down at work this month. You may think you are doing a good job, but driving a bus at 70mph through built-up areas could cost you your job. Then again, probably not.

Virgo *(Aug 24 - Sep 23)*

Is your Barton Hill high-rise getting you down? Are you dreaming of getting away from it all? Perhaps to hotter climates, with plenty of sand and lots of activities to keep you occupied? If you are a member of the Territorial Army, you could soon be on your way – just don't forget to pack your gas mask.

Libra *(Sep 24 - Oct 23)*

You need to learn to wind down before the stress of the city kills you. Don't know how? How about the City Centre Sauna on Stokes Croft where a full 'massage' and a pint can be yours from £50. On a budget? Try Portland Square where executive relief can be yours for a mere £20.

 Scorpio *(Oct 24 - Nov 22)*

Your boiler's broken down. Remember the old adage, if you want a job done properly then do it yourself. Why pay a CORGI-registered engineer a fortune when B&Q Longwell Green can provide you with all the parts you need. Sure the whole street is stinking of gas, but just sit back and think of the savings.

 Sagittarius *(Nov 23 - Dec 21)*

You have fruitlessly spent a fortune recently on scratch cards, lottery tickets and 20p grab-a-teddy machines. Never mind, Lady Luck is about to show you her hand this month. Well, to be more accurate, she will show you her middle finger as some prat's attempt at DIY results in your house being blown up.

 Capricorn *(Dec 22 - Jan 20)*

As the ancient Korean philosopher, It-Chee-Chin once said, "go west my child and seek your fortune". Unfortunately, he was not referring to Weston Pier where you are guaranteed to lose a fortune. Six for the Ghost Train? The only thing that's frightening is the price.

April

Isambard Kingdom Brunel

b. Apr 9th 1806 - d. Sep 15th 1859

Being born in Portsmouth would generally exclude someone from being classed as a Bristolian, but it is fair to say that Isambard Kingdom Brunel has been adopted by Bristol as one of its own. With some of his greatest works residing in the city, he helped put Bristol on the map for something other than slave trading. Indeed, without his legacy, hoards of burger-munching American tourists would get no further than Bath before heading back to London.

Brunel's connection with Bristol began after he won a competition to design a bridge to span the Avon Gorge. Through his work on the Clifton Suspension Bridge, he became friendly with the Merchant Venturers, which led to him being appointed chief engineer of the Great Western Railway, and building the Bristol to London railway as well as Temple Meads station.

Not content with building tunnels, bridges, and railways, he also turned his hand to ships, of which he built three, the *SS Great Western*, *SS Great Britain*, and *SS Great Eastern*. It was while working on the *SS Great Eastern* that his health deteriorated and, at the age of just 53, he had a stroke and died shortly afterwards.

Deemed the greatest and most versatile engineer of all time, he was backed by Jeremy Clarkson in the BBC competition *Greatest Ever Briton* and despite leading the contest most of the way, he eventually became runner up to Churchill (the war-time Prime Minister, not the dog from the car insurance advert).

Up the Gas!

On April 26th 1986, a crowd of 3,576 spectators witnessed Bristol Rovers' last-ever game at Eastville Stadium. It was a 1-1 draw with Chesterfield, bringing to an end Rovers' 89 year tenure at the stadium. Ironically, it was also in April of 1897 that Rovers played their first-ever match at the stadium – a 5-0 drubbing at the hands of Aston Villa. Sadly no film of this historic match exists, as this was in the days before *Soccer Night* – or the good old days.

Eastville Stadium had a unique feel to it. The close proximity to the Gas Works saw the club given the nickname 'The Gas' and their supporters, 'Gasheads'. Eastville was the only ground to ever have had flowerbeds behind the goals, though the task of trying to keep hundreds of steel toe-capped 'Tote End Boot Boys' out of the geraniums eventually proved too difficult.

But football was not the only sport at Eastville Stadium. Many people have fond memories of watching greyhound racing, and, for a short time, motorcycle speedway. However, once Rovers left, the stadium was doomed. The last remaining stand was demolished in October 1998 to make way for IKEA.

Whether it was roaring on the Rovers, losing money on the dogs or marvelling at the largest Hofmeister sign in the civilised world, a trip to Eastville Stadium was a vastly more pleasurable experience than wandering around a giant blue carbuncle looking at flat pack furniture. The smell of gas has long since departed, replaced by the smell of cheap hotdogs, Swedish furniture and the exhaust fumes of a thousand cars trying to exit at junction 2 of the M32.

A cup o' tea and a slice o' cake

April sees the re-opening of a whole bundle of facilities closed for the winter season. Of all the things to do this month, the top has to be taking a boat up the River Avon to Beeses Tea Gardens. However, like the proverbial single swallow, it's not quite summer yet – so bring your pac-a-mac.

Opened in 1846 to provide refreshments for travellers on the Conham ferry after their long and arduous journey twenty feet across from Hanham, it took its name from the captain of the ferry at that time, Mr Bees Tea Rooms. The ferry still runs and is the oldest river ferry crossing on the River Avon – though don't attempt to drive your car onto it, as it's basically just a big rowing boat.

The majority of visitors arrive by charted excursion on the *Bristol Packet* after cruising up from central Bristol. Admittedly, you could sail to France quicker, but as it is mainly full of pensioners and tourists who have nothing better to do with their day, there's no rush. What could be more relaxing than meandering along the waterways, past the derelict Post Office building on Cattle Market Road, up the Feeder Canal breathing in the fumes from the main road while enjoying the never-ending vista of industrial units that line its banks. Just stay beneath deck till you're past Netham Lock and it'll all be lovely.

However you get there, Beeses is definitely worth a visit. While the rooms are open all year round, they really get swinging from Easter. They offer some excellent food, indulgent cream teas and most importantly of all, some decent beers.

Dear IKB

As a suburban professional who commutes into town on a daily basis, I'm finding the cost of running my Mondeo GLX increasingly difficult to afford. Mostly it's the extortionate price of petrol that's starting to take its toll on my finances. My five credit cards are now all maxed out and I'm already on my third re-mortgage. What can I do to reduce my transportation costs before I become bankrupt?

Richard, Emersons Green

IKB SAYS:

As an engineer, I am not a man who is able to comment on matters of finance. I always managed to find some gullible investor or other to finance my projects, making sure that I kept hold of my own money in case the whole thing went tits up.

Your transport problems however, I can help you with. There is a one-word answer to your dilemma: steam. While I know not of the technical details of this Mondeo you speak of, if it's not steam-driven it must be about as useful as a locomotive powered by electricity.

I think you'll find that filling the fuel tank of your vehicle with water will be fairly cheap. Steam is the clean fuel of the future – forgetting the coal fire you need to create it, of course.

Famous Bristolians Who Actually Aren't

Tony Robinson *(London)*
James Redmond *(London)*
Nick Park *(Preston)*
Tony Bullimore *(Essex)*
John Cabot *(Genoa, Italy)*
Vicky Pollard *(Darkly Noone)*

April

Glamorous Bristol Streets

Hollywood Road
Jamaica Street
California Road
St Lucia Close
Trowbridge Road

Popular BBC Radio Bristol Shows

Sounds of Brass *(Sunday 19:00)*
Swingers and Singers *(Sunday 20:00)*
Bristol Community FM *(Sunday 03:00)*
Dave Barrett *(Weekdays 09:00)*

MAY

God helps those who help themselves
(try telling that one at Bristol Magistrates Court)

At the start of this month Council transport officials will publicly deny having introduced congestion charging to the city, claiming if they had it would certainly cost more than ten pounds. The police will warn the motoring public to be on the lookout for a man wearing a fluorescent donkey jacket with pockets stuffed with ten pound notes, last seen near the Galleries.

In a bid to reduce rush hour traffic, the City Council will this month launch its latest transport plan: Swim to Work. With several waterways flowing into central Bristol, it is hoped people will take to heart the Saxon name of the city, '*meeting place by the river*', and join up with fellow commuters on the banks before taking a steady crawl into the Centre. Costume sharing will be optional.

A-to-Z will announce this month that new maps being drawn up for Bristol will see the official adoption of Turbo Island as a place-name. In recognition of the tramps, drunks, and cheap cider that gave the area its name, a set of bronze statues will be installed at the green site. Thomas Cook will later announce package holidays to Turbo Island, beginning in Autumn 2008.

A builder will face prosecution from Bristol City Council this month for building a new hotel at Canons Marsh without first gaining planning permission. The Withywood man, a semi-professional board games player, will enrage planning officials after they hear he has located a hotel next to @Bristol while playing the Bristol edition of *Monopoly* at the South Bristol regional championships.

May

 Aquarius *(Jan 21 - Feb 19)*

Why not sit out on the balcony overlooking the Bristol waterfront and enjoy a bottle of wine with your partner. Watch passing people on boats look over at you in envy as they see the million pound luxury apartment behind you. A perfect way to spend the evening, as long as no one sees the ladder you used to climb up to the balcony and the owner doesn't return home.

 Pisces *(Feb 20 - Mar 20)*

Any month that contains a Bank Holiday is great, but May is exceptional as it contains two. But why settle for just two extra long weekends? Phone in sick on all the other Mondays and you can have a month full of them. Go on, get your fishing rod out and get down the Feeder, my son!

 Aries *(Mar 21 - Apr 20)*

As the unemployment rate in Bristol starts to rise again, you manage to get yourself fired after your boss catches you fishing down the Feeder when you should be working. Never mind, you may have no job and no money, but look on the bright side – your weekends have just got even longer.

Taurus *(Apr 21 - May 21)*

Looking for an exciting family day out that's close to the Bristol area? Why not ignore all the warning signs and take a stroll across the mud flats at Brean Down. The kids will love becoming part of a major sea rescue, with the added bonus of a helicopter ride thrown in. And best of all, it's free, so you can do it all over again the next day.

 Gemini *(May 22 - Jun 21)*

It's about time you started to show your partner some support. She decides to enter the 5K Race for Life and all you can do is take the mickey. Instead of poking fun, why don't you get yourself up to the Downs and bloody well cheer her on (along with the other 10,000 scantily clad ladies). I thought that would change your mind!

 Cancer *(Jun 22 - Jul 23)*

Now the weather is picking up and everyone in Bristol seems to be enjoying a barbecue, it's time to dust off your old set, dig out the charcoal and invite some friends around. Summer's never really fully arrived until you have managed to poison most of your nearest and dearest. Rare chicken, anyone?

 Leo *(Jul 24 – Aug 23)*

So the powers that be have decided to put up the bus fares in Bristol again. An unreliable service that takes ages to arrive and when it finally does the driver is rude and the inside is filthy. Is it ever worth it? Well, of course it is, with the arrival of the warm weather comes the best entertainment of all – wasp on the top deck.

 Virgo *(Aug 24 – Sep 23)*

Summer will soon be here so maybe it's time to get fit. Ditch the unreliable bus service, leave the car at home and make a vow to start cycling to work. Nothing could be more invigorating than pedalling along the Feeder, the wind in your hair, fresh air in your lungs and a juggernaut two inches behind your back wheel blasting its horn.

 Libra *(Sep 24 – Oct 23)*

Things are not coming together as you had planned, so in hindsight it was probably a mistake to throw away those assembly instructions for the furniture you purchased at IKEA in Eastville. Never mind, it's testimony to your resourcefulness that you can still complete the job with screws to spare – even if the wardrobe is sloping at 45°.

May

 Scorpio *(Oct 24 - Nov 22)*

There aren't many retreats from the concrete jungle that is Bristol, but the Downs has to be the best one. You can get away from the strife of city life by enjoying a stroll around the grass, a cup of tea in the bogs, or an ice cream by the Sea Walls. Now just feel that stress leaving your body. Hang on – isn't that your car being towed away?

 Sagittarius *(Nov 23 - Dec 21)*

Career-wise you have spent more time crawling than a 12-month-old baby. Well perhaps now is the time to jet off from Bristol International Airport and take a well-deserved break. Stop worrying who will make your boss's tea. You just concentrate on getting a tan as brown as your tongue.

 Capricorn *(Dec 22 - Jan 20)*

Getting on the first rung of the mortgage ladder can be tough at the best of times, but in Bristol, where the house prices are higher than a top floor flat in Barton Hill, you have got no chance. Perhaps it's time to look a little further out of the area – Newcastle for instance.

May

Colin Pillinger

b. May 9th 1943

Despite looking more like Worzel Gummidge with his thinking head on than a space boffin, Professor Colin Pillinger is the boldest and most determined planetary scientist to ever have graced the streets of Kingswood. Inspired by reading *Dan Dare* comics, Pillinger grew up wanting to become a footballer. Luckily for science, his dreams of playing for Rovers came to nothing.

Pillinger spent the early years of his career analysing Moon rocks brought back from the Moon by the Apollo 11 astronauts. But it was while in his position as Professor of Planetary Sciences at the Open University that he came up with the idea for Beagle 2. One hell of a lot of badgering and blagging later and the project was given the green light. From the very inception to the bitter end Pillinger remained the driving force behind the Mars-bound lander, and it was his drive and determination that got it off the ground.

Of course it's no secret that the Beagle 2 mission didn't go exactly to plan. Despite managing to make it to the red planet, it fell at the last hurdle. The European Space Agency conducted a report into what went wrong with Beagle 2, the summary being: it got there, it just didn't land all that well.

Whatever you think of Pillinger, he was responsible for building Britain's first interplanetary spacecraft, and all for the cost of a round of coffee at NASA. More importantly, in doing so, he put science and space exploration back into the public eye. Who knows, maybe because of that, somewhere amongst Kingswood's mean streets lurks a Pillinger protégé ready to succeed.

Aaaaaaaaa… SPLAT!

On May 8th 1885, 22-year-old Sarah Ann Henley entered the history books after she jumped off the Clifton Suspension Bridge and survived. Devastated after her boyfriend had written to her telling her that their engagement was off, she headed up to Clifton and jumped off the bridge.

Instead of following the Wile E. Coyote path of straight down to the bottom and instant death, she was instead saved by the petticoats under her dress, which acted as a form of parachute allowing her to float away from the water. She even managed a somersault on the way down, but lost marks for her landing – hard, in thick mud on the banks of the river.

Two people who had witnessed her fall managed to drag her from the mud and a passing doctor used his medical skills to diagnose that she probably needed to be rushed to hospital. Unfortunately, rushing anyone anywhere in those days was not straightforward.

A passing cabbie was asked by the police to take her to the BRI, but the unsympathetic driver, more worried about the condition of his cab than the state of her internal organs, refused on account she was covered in mud. In the end she was rushed to the BRI by stretcher.

While recovering in hospital, she received offers of marriage and even the chance of a tour, though recreating that epic jump every night strangely didn't appeal to her. Despite making a full recovery she eventually died anyway in 1948 at the age of 85.

2008AD

While most boys' involvement with comics ends by the time they've left school and discovered beer and girls, this event is still sure to be a sell-out as geeks from around the world make an annual pilgrimage from their bedrooms to the Bristol International Comic Expo.

Held at the British Empire and Commonwealth Exhibition Hall, this three-day event brings together the biggest names in the comic industry, from world famous artists and exhibitors to the new kids on the block (comic artists, not the former 80s boy band).

Whether you enjoy a gentle chuckle while reading about the antics of the Bash Street Kids in *The Beano*, or prefer seeing someone being chopped into a thousand pieces in a manga comic, there's sure to be something to suit all tastes. Just don't forget your credit card, as that elusive back issue you've been after since 1979 isn't going to be selling for the cover price.

As well as being able to listen to people talk all about their life in comics, you will be able to look at comics, buy comics, debate the best comics, and go to the comic awards. If your partner isn't too into comics, it's probably best to go alone.

So get your secret Superman outfit out and take the opportunity to dress up here, nobody will even look twice – unless of course you're catching the night bus home afterwards, in which case you are most likely destined to get a good kicking – which won't look good in superhero circles.

May

Dear IKB

With the new series of *Big Brother* now upon us, do you have any advice on how I can juggle my life around so I can spend 24-7 watching it? As it is the best reality show on television I don't want to miss one single second of it. Please, please, please can you apply your huge intellect to my problem?

Darren, Stockwood

IKB SAYS:

Firstly may I say that the only thing you should be doing with reality is getting a grip on it - firmly, and with both hands. As to juggling your life around to enable you to sit in front of a picture box day and night, that shouldn't be difficult as it sounds like you don't have a life anyway.

But failing common sense managing to penetrate your skull, I suggest you spend some time attempting to design a railway system based around the standard gauge of 4ft 8½in that would allow for as smooth an operation of trains at high speeds as my discarded 7ft gauge system.

The reasoning behind this is - much like you – simple. It should prove, even to you, that just because something is very popular it doesn't actually make it any good. If you want my advice, forget Big Brother *and try reading a book instead. You can read, can't you?*

May

Facts About Bristol City Centre

The concrete covered River Frome that the majority of the Bristolian public would like to see re-opened, creating a far more attractive Centre, actually no longer exists. The City Council sold it off back in the heatwave year of 1977 to pay for more traffic lights. Hence their reluctance to follow public opinion in creating a continental-style waterway.

As big and strong as the few trees growing on the Centre are, believe it or not none of them actually grew through the concrete slabs. A long, long time ago on a Centre far far away, there used to be soil, flowers, bushes, and even some grass. No, honestly.

At 2:30am on a Saturday night / Sunday morning, the Centre taxi queue is the only human grouping on earth that can be seen from the international space station with the naked eye. This cattle-like horde of kebab-carrying bodies also makes the Centre statistically the best location in Bristol on which to run over a drunken idiot in a Ben Sherman shirt.

The roof of the Bristol Hippodrome, one of the very few buildings in the Centre not actually a pub or an office, completely opens up to allow big name stars to fly directly in and out of the venue via helicopter, thus avoiding the hordes of baying fans at the stage door. Sadly, there has been no need to use this entrance for nearly twenty years, not since the last Hinge and Bracket concert.

JUNE

A Bristolian's home is his castle
(particularly if it's a black one in Brislington)

Police will be called in after the disappearance of a cyclist taking part in Bristol's Biggest Bike Ride this month. Two weeks will pass until they will be found cycling around the upper deck of the QE2 three-hundred miles off the coast of North America after getting confused between Clevedon in Somerset and Cleveland, Ohio.

Trustees of St Mary Redcliffe, one of Bristol's most historic churches, will become fed up with replacing vandalised windows this month and decide to install modern replacements. However, replacing all of the historic stained glass with UPVC double-glazing will cause something of a stir and result in several people writing letters to the *Evening Post*.

Following a break of twenty years, powerboats are set to return to Bristol's fashionable dockland area this month, but not for racing – for use as water taxis. However, the plans could hit the wall before they set off, as existing boat owners will oppose the harbour speed limit increase from the current 6mph to 150mph. Swimming commuters will be advised to wear luminous swim caps.

The hottest summer since 1976 will hit the city this month, bringing a mini heat wave. As people struggle to cope with the high temperatures, First Bus will be forced to introduce a strict dress code, banning man-made fibres after three passengers on the top deck of a number 44 at Lawrence Hill spontaneously combust while waiting for the driver to change.

June

 Aquarius *(Jan 21 - Feb 19)*

Inspired by programmes such as *A Place in the Sun* and *Relocation, Relocation, Relocation,* you have decided to move away from Bristol to make a new life for yourself. But you are harbouring fears: how will you keep in contact with friends, how will you adapt to the new way of living a life by the sea? I wouldn't worry too much – it's only Weston-super-Mare.

 Pisces *(Feb 20 - Mar 20)*

You are thinking of getting on the property ladder. It's an exciting time. Where do you plan to live? Clifton, Redland, Westbury-on-Trym? However, once you've calculated how much you can actually borrow and you've checked the price of your dream pad you might be better suited looking in the garden shed section of B&Q.

 Aries *(Mar 21 - Apr 20)*

Heartfelt of Hartcliffe, you have been taking on everyone's problems recently and have been a real shoulder to cry on. But who listens to your fears and worries? Maybe the time is right to share your problems with your nearest and dearest. Think again, no one likes a whinging git.

- 76 -

 Taurus *(Apr 21 - May 21)*

You need to keep your temper under control, as you only end up hurting yourself. Remember the time you head-butted a speed camera? There's an old saying, "The pen is mightier than the sword." If things are really getting under your skin, don't lash out – instead write a letter to the *Evening Post*. There you go – painless, if totally pointless.

Gemini *(May 22 - Jun 21)*

Take care in dangerous situations this month when not everything may be as it first appears. While on the face of it you think you are a hero for attempting to rescue an elderly lady after she reverses her car though a shop window, the reality is simply ruining a day's filming of *Casualty*.

 Cancer *(Jun 22 - Jul 23)*

As the summer solstice arrives in Bristol, you must resist the urge to dance around in the buff whilst rubbing the blood of several sacrificed chickens onto those around you – particularly if you want to keep your job at Miss Millies.

June

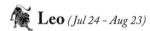

Leo *(Jul 24 – Aug 23)*

This month, fortune favours the brave. So stop being such a chicken and ask out that girl you really fancy. What's holding you back? The fear of rejection or her really big boyfriend? What's the worse that can happen? Time can mend a broken heart and the BRI can repair a broken jaw.

June

Virgo *(Aug 24 – Sep 23)*

Communication matters should be high on your agenda this month. It's been a while since you've had a letter published in the *Evening Post*, probably a matter of weeks. Why not take time to rectify this by penning another bitter attack against single mothers, sex shops, or even those bastards that keep stealing your bike?

Libra *(Sep 24 – Oct 23)*

While some people live their lives like they are travelling in the fast lane of the M32, you prefer to live yours like you are travelling in the slow lane pulling a caravan to Brean. Well, now is the time to cut free and get a bit reckless. Go on, go out and get a tattoo, get drunk and have a fight. Mind you, don't forget to put your cardigan on first, as it could get nippy.

HOROSCOPES

by Rose Green

 Scorpio *(Oct 24 – Nov 22)*

Have you been neglecting the kids? Why not set aside some quality time for them this month. Treat them to a day trip. There are loads of things to do in and around Bristol. Why not take out a mortgage and go to the Zoo, or how about a visit to @Bristol. What, you have been to both of these? Well bloody well go again! That's what the rest of us end up doing.

 Sagittarius *(Nov 23 – Dec 21)*

You've always been a quick thinker, which helps you out when your wife comes home early from work one day to catch you in her best slacks. "Wrong Trousers Day, love!" – who can resist the call of charity. Let's just hope she doesn't notice one of her thongs is missing as well.

 Capricorn *(Dec 22 – Jan 20)*

Having Mars in Uranus this month could lead to a rather embarrassing situation should you end up in the casualty department at the BRI again. Stay vigilant and remember what your mother always told you: Always make sure you're wearing clean pants, and never stick chocolate bars where the sun don't shine.

Damien Hirst

b. Jun 7ᵗʰ 1965

One of the most famous artists of the 1990s, you could be forgiven for thinking that Hirst was merely a butcher without a shop. With his collections of pickled lumps of dead animals in glass cases making him a multi-millionaire, you can't help thinking that maybe banging a few assorted offcuts into jars could've saved Dewhurst from going under.

Away from the formaldehyde, Hirst is also renowned for painting coloured dots, another nice little money-spinning line, despite the fact that he doesn't actually paint them all himself. Apparently he once claimed he "…couldn't be f**cking arsed doing it". But who needs to when it'll sell for a fortune anyway. Mind you, if you want a picture of coloured dots in your front room it would probably be a lot cheaper to stick a twister mat on your wall.

Despite such apathy, in 2002 Hirst was persuaded by fellow Bristolian Professor Colin Pillinger to paint a pattern of dots for use on the Mars-bound Beagle 2 spacecraft. The artwork was to be used to calibrate the craft's cameras once it had landed. However, after the ship smashed into the Martian surface there wasn't a lot of need for calibration anymore. Despite seemingly being marooned on the surface of Mars, no doubt this artwork will miraculously appear for sale on eBay at some point in the near future.

Depending on your perspective on art, Hirst is both an utter genius and one of the most important people to appear on the British art scene in recent years, or just shit. You decide.

June

Samuel Plimsoll

b. Feb 10ᵗʰ 1824 – d. Jun 3ʳᵈ 1898

Rather than being the inventor of daps as his name may suggest, former politician Plimsoll invented lines on the side of ships. But not just any old line, but a collection of lines to mark the maximum level to which a ship's keel could be submerged, depending on its contents and where in the world it was. Now simply known as the Plimsoll Line, it has since been adopted by every seafaring nation in the world.

Plimsoll was instrumental in campaigning for legislation to stop ship owners from overloading their poorly maintained vessels (nicknamed 'Coffin Ships' by the sailors) to the point where they would sink in heavy seas – something apparently not a problem when you're heavily insured. It wasn't an easy battle as the wealthy Victorian merchants of the time held powerful sway over politicians, and 'corporate social responsibility' wasn't exactly the business buzzword it is today. He was often ridiculed and dismissed as buffoon.

However, Plimsoll, known commonly as ' the sailor's friend', finally saw the introduction of the Plimsoll Line in 1876. Countless thousands of potential deaths were avoided and the seas were safer to sail. Well, apart from sea monsters, pirates, and the Bermuda Triangle, of course.

To commemorate his great achievements, and as a thank you for his nautical legacy from a maritime city, Bristol remembers Plimsoll with a bronze bust located beside a busy main road.

June

Up the Smoke

Despite the high-ticket cost, overcrowding, and inevitable delays, it's still hard to contemplate not being able to get a train from Bristol to London. In fact, since the route opened for business on June 30th 1841, it's been carrying Bristolians to the capital, not one of which ever saw the point of Didcot Parkway.

While Temple Meads station itself was opened in 1840 you could only initially get a train as far as Bath, which would've meant one hell of a walk up the A4 if you had a meeting to get to. Chances are you wouldn't have made it for brunch.

The original Temple Meads building is now a Grade I listed building and the oldest railway terminus in the world. It's a perfect example of how even utilitarian buildings in the Victorian age oozed style and class. The building we use as the station today wasn't built until the 1870s, eventually replacing Brunel's original terminus completely when that was closed in 1965. But even the 'new' building walks all over anything else around – particularly Parkway Station.

Temple Meads stands tall and proud as a symbol of all that the city had achieved in Brunel's time. Parkway on the other hand is an aluminium cowshed where people catch the train to Wales. Which is why when people walk out of Temple Meads and look for a taxi they queue in a dignified fashion and at Parkway there is always an almighty scramble as people run past each other to grab taxis from the rank.

Saddle Sore-a-Rama

This month will see thousands of cyclists leave the payments and take to the roads for the 15th annual Biggest Bike Ride. It doesn't matter if you fancy yourself as the next Chris Boardman or have the physical appearance of Stan Boardman; if you ride a bike worth £1,000 or a bike with stabilisers and a shopping basket on the front – the main aim of the event is to raise loads of money for a host of important charities.

People of all shapes and sizes are welcome to take part, and if you are unable manage to ride or are just too damn lazy, spectators are also welcome to come along and offer their support to the riders, although shouting "fat bottom girls, get on your bikes and ride" may result in you getting a punch in the face.

The routes usually range from a gentle eight-mile family-friendly jaunt to a not very family-friendly, lung-busting thirty-eight miler. Don't forget though, you are actually expected to ride these routes. Following behind in the car while your bike is strapped to the boot is not technically taking part – it's called cheating. Also, if you're attempting the long one, remember to take a puncture repair kit, unless you want to end up pushing a bike nineteen miles home.

If nothing else, this event provides you with the opportunity to raise loads of money while enjoying the fresh air and meeting lots of new people. Just don't blame us when your entire body is covered in Lycra burns and you end up walking like a cowboy for the next three weeks.

June

Dear IKB

I am now nearing the age where I can afford to drive without using one of those special screwdriver keys to start other people's cars. I would like to know whether, in your opinion, I should splash out on the dreamy Nova SRi with compulsory steel radials and portable boogie box in the passenger seat or go for the suburban dream that is a 1995 Ford Fiesta, and which apparently comes with a radio already installed.

Trev

IKB SAYS:

The male coming of age is an important time of life that is full of change. Not only does the change from boy to man mean you are no longer small enough to clean chimneys, but your facial hair grows, you develop a liking for ale, and you are deemed responsible enough to take control of a powered vehicle – ideally not after extreme 'liking' of ale.

It is a magical and wondrous time in a man's life and an ideal one to attract the attention of the opposite sex – before you get fat, bald, and lazy. It is for this reason that your vehicle should be selected carefully, the musical device you choose and the music that emanates from it.

So my recommendation to you is simple – get yourself a steam engine. The 'pulling power' of a good steam locomotive far outweighs any modern motorised vehicle. Sound-wise you should load up a few carriages with a Welsh male voice choir singing a medley of current popular hits. If that doesn't make people stop and stare as you pass through platform 5 at Temple Meads, I'll eat my hat – and by golly it's a big one.

June

Living Bristolians
(we couldn't be bothered to write about)

James May *(Captain Slow)*
Chris Morris *(Satirist)*
Julie Burchill *(Bitchy columnist)*
Fred Wedlock *(Raconteur)*
Sophie Anderton *(Model turned reality TV regular)*

Bristol Songs By *The Wurzels*

Virtue et Industrial
One for the Bristol City
Moonlight on the Malago
Avonmouth Mary

Dead Bristolians
(we couldn't be bothered to write about)

Elizabeth Blackwell *(First female doctor)*
Thomas Chatterton *(Suicidal romantic poet)*
Edward Colston *(Philanthropic slave trader)*
William Friese-Green *(Film pioneer)*
Robert Southey *(Poet laureate)*

June

JULY

A leopard can never change its spots
(so don't ask for your money back at the zoo)

Bristol's Urban Beach will return to Redcliffe Wharf, but following complaints of exclusion in 2007 this year it will be promoted as a half naturist resort (half the beach not half the clothes). While organisers ask people to consider the environment and take their summer break at Redcliffe, nobody will expect the arrival of a coach-load of naked Polish pensioners.

The popular outdoor cinema will return to Queen Square, promising a classic film from a local award-winning movie legend. Thousands of picnic-carrying Cary Grant fans will arrive expecting *North by Northwest* or *Bringing Up Baby*, but uproar will break out amongst the jugs of Pimms once the film starts and they discover it's in fact *Saturday Night Beaver* starring Cathy Barry.

A WWII German U-boat will be discovered in the docks during the harbour festival after several drunken members of a hen party stagger into the water outside a nightclub. The German crew who had been silently waiting for further instructions – since 1941 – did not know the war was over and believing the drunken women hitting their ship were suicide bombers, decide to finally surrender.

As a grand finale to the harbour festival, a giant free barbeque will be held. To help get it lit, a petrol can is emptied over it, which sees a massive blaze quickly take hold. Unfortunately, the barbeque is being held onboard Cabot's wooden replica ship, the *Matthew*, which goes up in smoke before sinking. People attempt to launch a desperate salvage bid but sadly no chicken wings will be saved.

July

Aquarius *(Jan 21 - Feb 19)*

Abandon all hope, as the four horsemen of the apocalypse descend on Bristol bringing with them flood, plague and pestilence. Well, alright – it's just the kids breaking up from school for the summer holidays, but you can bet that they'll will be twice as destructive.

Pisces *(Feb 20 - Mar 20)*

Making up your mind has never been your strong point. Remember the time that bus driver asked you if you wanted a single or a return? Oh, the dilemma! But this month you really do need to be more decisive, or you won't get out of Brislington before Christmas. So, deal or no deal?

Aries *(Mar 21 - Apr 20)*

The summer has arrived and it's time to escape the Bristol rat race and venture to foreign shores served by EasyJet. What better way to experience a different culture than spending every night surrounded by drunken Brits, eating English food and watching premiership football. Garlic bread?

July

 **Taurus** *(Apr 21 - May 21)*

You're proud that you are not a sheep and your individuality means you don't like to go with the flow. Mind you, driving your car down the M32 in the wrong direction is taking things a tad too far. Now, keeping your eyes firmly on the road, please repeat after me – BAAAA.

Gemini *(May 22 - Jun 21)*

"Irene Smedley smells of shit" – well that's according to graffiti on a disused pub in St Phillips anyway. However, unless your name is Irene Smedley, this should be of no concern to you. Best concentrate on getting your life back together following your painful divorce and the shocking discovery you haven't even made it into the first round of the Reader's Digest prize draw.

Cancer *(Jun 22 - Jul 23)*

Is the pressure at work getting to you? Too much to do and not enough time to do it? Why not delegate more of your work. Unless of course you're an Air Traffic Controller at Bristol International Airport. Best not leave the landing of that Boeing 757 from Menorca to a temp from Office Angels.

July

 **HOROSCOPES** *by Rose Green*

Leo *(Jul 24 - Aug 23)*

A bit of sunshine and out come the shorts and off goes your shirt. Only then do you realise how skinny your body really is. Maybe it's time to join one of those £700 a year exclusive health clubs that are popping up all over the Bristol area. Probably cheaper just to put your shirt back on.

Virgo *(Aug 24 - Sep 23)*

Sometimes it's difficult to keep our deepest desires and fantasies hidden. You have always fantasised about having sex on an exotic beach, though the cost has prohibited you. Well, with a bit of imagination it needn't cost the earth. Why not take your partner Severn Beach. If you keep your eyes closed and don't breathe in you could almost be in the Caribbean.

Libra *(Sep 24 - Oct 23)*

Money will feature heavily for you this month, as you will be swamped with interested buyers for your flash motor. It's annoying that none of them are offering close to what it's worth, but even more annoying that it wasn't you who put it in *Trade-It* for £50 in the first place.

 HOROSCOPES *by Rose Green*

 ## Scorpio *(Oct 24 - Nov 22)*

Summer lovin' had me a blast, summer loving happened so fast, I met a girl crazy for me, just my luck to meet a loony. Be warned this month, with the hot summer sun shining down on the fashionable waterfront drinking holes any attention from the opposite sex could just be alcohol-induced madness.

 ## Sagittarius *(Nov 23 - Dec 21)*

Summer days driftin' away, to uh, oh the summer nights – are full of drunken idiots spilling kebabs into the wonderful Centre fountains. No wonder they don't ever work properly. Never mind, it'll soon be Christmas. Ordered your turkey yet?

 ## Capricorn *(Dec 22 - Jan 20)*

Do you feel lucky? Well, do you ya, punk? Your stars this month suggest you should. Why don't you put it to the test by base jumping off Cabot Tower, or even more deadly, trying to cross the Centre during rush hour? Much like a medieval witch dunking: if you survive you must be a true jammer.

July

Justin Lee Collins

b. Jul 28th 1974

Half-man half-hair, JLC is the Bristolian bastard lovechild of Davina McCall and Captain Caveman, with a native accent of such undiluted strength it's almost a parody of itself. An incredible improviser and great Tom Jones impersonator, he has a unique ability to 'filth up' any given situation and yet still manage to keep even your granny smiling. Rock on!

But, like the wait for a bus in Bristol, his current mainstream success has been a long time coming. After leaving school at 15 with no qualifications, he became comedic aide, Harry Helium on the Dave Barrett radio phone-in show during the late 1980s. Jump forward twenty years and he is still playing a giant curry flavoured Twiglet. Bad times.

However, things started to look up after a successful stint presenting the digital spin-off of BBC's *Strictly Come Dancing* (despite getting axed for a bird with a big fringe for the second series). Unusually for a presenter, he left the BBC to join Channel 4 (at that time known as Jimmy Carr television).

JLC was an immediate hit, first through his hilarious interviewing of celebrities on *The Games* and then with his popular *Bring Back* series, which has included *Grange Hill*, *The A-Team*, and *Dallas*, where he rarely managed to bring back anyone, but had great fun chasing them around. Since then, his co-hosting of Channel 4's award-winning *Friday Night Project* has made him the talk of the town. But even with all his fame, his riches, and his hair, he remains a firm resident of the city. Good times.

Charles Stephens

b. c1863 - d. Jul 11th 1920

Known as the 'Demon Barber of Bristol', Stephens gained notoriety for being a not just a dab hand with a razor, but also a part-time daredevil. Once he realised that cutting hair alone wasn't going to bring in enough money to feed his football team of kids, he decided to turn his hand to performing death-defying stunts to earn a bit of extra cash.

Seemingly fearless (or stupid), Stephens had a go at parachuting, wrestling with lions, and even allowed people to shoot at cubes of sugar resting on his head. However, as none of these efforts really generated enough money, he decided to attempt the ultimate stunt – riding a barrel over Niagara Falls. Despite being warned by many not to try it, Stephens rolled up at the Falls with his own heavyweight oak barrel, convinced he knew better.

He was certain that the secret to success was to get inside the barrel and strap his arms down. Not only that, but as an extra precaution to keep him upright, in true cartoon style, he fixed a large anvil to his feet. This was a plan that simply could not fail – at least in his own mind.

Clearly Stephens was no rocket scientist and what he had failed to realise was the kinetic energy generated by a large anvil after it had fallen 53 metres. Once he hit the water the anvil went straight through the bottom of the barrel, taking most of Stephens with it to the bottom of the river. Some hours later the barrel resurfaced – with just one of Stephens' arms still attached. Ouch.

July

Animal Magic

First opened to the public on July 11th 1836, Bristol Zoo is the fifth oldest zoo in the world and has long been a favourite day out for Bristolians, their families, and the Welsh. In the Victorian era the emphasis was as much on social and recreational use as it was animals. There were sporting events, bands playing, and even boating trips on the lake.

During WWII, the metal shortage saw all the bars removed from cages. Whilst good for the war effort it was surprisingly bad for visitor numbers. It was later decided it would be safer to evacuate many of the animals, which resulted in chaos at Temple Meads, as hundreds of balaclava-clad penguins carrying suitcases tried to board trains for Devon.

It's also a little known fact that over 70% of the chimpanzees at Bristol Zoo have equity cards and have appeared in various PG Tips adverts over the years. However, visitors are discouraged from throwing tea bags into the enclosures and shouting "the piano's on me foot Dad, the piano's on me foot".

Served by a reasonable bus service (for Bristol), driving to the zoo should be avoided. Parking at the zoo in peak season is simple – you can't. Instead you are forced to park in a specially designated area opposite the zoo called 'The Downs'. When parking here you should take care to follow the directions – otherwise you may find yourself careering across the wrong part of the Downs, knocking over joggers, kite flyers, and Frisbee fans alike.

July

Ashton Court Festival

From a series of small events held back in 1974, Ashton Court Festival grew beyond recognition into Bristol's most loved weekend. Despite being once proudly hailed as Europe's largest free festival, a nominal entry fee was introduced several years ago to help cover the cost of organising the event.

For many it seems this is where its original vibe started to be chipped away. First came the entry fee, then the fence, then somebody decided to close the Clifton Suspension Bridge for the duration of the event. The thought of the good people of Bristol not being able to use his bridge would surely have Brunel spinning in his grave – were he not dead.

Undoubtedly worst of all, however, was the announcement that people would no longer be able to bring their own booze. For many, the festival meant nothing more than lying around all day demolishing a case of Blackthorn while listening to local bands. Queuing for hours on end to buy an over-priced pint in a wobbly glass was never going to be the same.

In 2007, it was doubtful whether the Festival would happen at all, but the dedicated team of volunteers worked their fingers to the bone to get it up and running. After a lot of hard graft and a few changes, the weekend got the green light. Shame – it chucked it down on Saturday night, and Sunday got cancelled anyway. This forced the company into liquidation and spelt the end. Will the weekend rise from the mud in 2008? I wouldn't hold your breath.

July

St Paul's Carnival

Running more or less continuously since 1968 when the first carnival paraded past the Mayor of Bristol, once a year this much-maligned area of Bristol deservedly takes centre stage as it puts on its spectacular annual carnival that the whole city can be proud of.

The problem is that due to the ever-increasing number of health and safety rules, each year it becomes more difficult and costly to stage such an event. Whereas years ago you just got up on a Saturday morning, set up some kick-ass sound system, decorated a few floats and started drinking and partying in the streets, these days you have to plan months in advance and make sure you are insured for every eventuality, from drunken fools getting knocked over by carnival floats to someone slipping on a discarded beer bottle.

Like the Ashton Court Festival, it's a shame that this event is struggling to survive. For many Bristolians attending it is the only chance they will ever get to sample curried goat, drink Red Stripe lager and listen to reggae music with a bass so deep it will have pensioners across Bristol scrambling for the Anderson shelter as they think Purdown Percy has started up again.

Of course, there is a very good possibility that the event will be cancelled once again, either due to even more red tape being introduced or possibly the great British summer weather, in which case you will have to stay at home and make do with an Asda curry, a can of Fosters and the *Best of UB40*.

July

Dear IKB

The other day I was travelling to work (by rail I hasten to add) and do you know it took me a whopping 6 hours, 15 minutes and 5 seconds and I was only going from Lawrence Hill to Temple Meads! Anyway it made me bloody late. In your day this would have been acceptable, but surely not in the 21st century. What do you think?

Sam, Speedwell

IKB SAYS:

Let me start by saying that there is some ambiguity over your name, as 'Sam' could relate to either a man or a woman in your cosmopolitan 21st century. However, as you mention 'work' in your letter, I can only assume you are a man – unless of course your husband had forgotten his lunch and you were making a special journey to ensure he received his sustenance, which would only be expected.

I myself was never late for work, as I never actually stopped working – well not until I dropped dead anyway. I think your problem is summed up in the place name: Lawrence Hill. Trains will always have trouble travelling up hills. What you need to do is build a tunnel straight through the hill. I estimate it will probably take anywhere between six and sixty years in total, depending on your engineering experience and ability to control unskilled labourers.

If by chance you do happen to be a woman, forget this advice. Just sit back and enjoy the journey – what else were you going to do with your day anyway?

July

Bristol Riots

Bristol Bridge *(1793)*
Queens Square *(1831)*
St Pauls *(1980)*
Hartcliffe *(1992)*

Suburban Anagrams

Kingswood – *I know dogs*
St George – *Gert egos*
Eastville – *Stale evil*
Bishopston – *No posh bits*
Southville – *Lush to vile*
Ashton Gate – *Not hate gas*
The Downs – *Shed town*
Speedwell – *Deep wells*
Westbury – *We try bus*
Sea Mills – *Is a smell*

Streets To Make Schoolboys Snigger

Cock Road
Gays Road
King Dick Lane

July

AUGUST

Bad news travels fast
(except in Bristol traffic)

Thousands of wellwishers will gather on the harbour side to see Tony Bullimore set sail on the recently re-built *Matthew* as he attempts to recreate Cabot's epic voyage to Newfoundland. Unfortunately, after some initial confusion over directions, the ship will travel a short distance in the wrong direction before colliding with the *SS Great Britain* and capsizing.

A controversial proposal to hold the International Balloon Fiesta indoors in a bid to guarantee the weather will outrage balloonists and spectators across the city this month. The decision to hold the event in the Mall Galleries in Broadmead will be announced just days beforehand, shocking both those planning to attend and the Mall retailers themselves.

As the new football season begins, Bristol Rovers are forced to admit their new stadium will be larger than originally thought, after a local resident returns home from holiday to find a row of seats installed in his back garden. In an act of goodwill, he is promised free tickets to all future home matches, although with no guarantee it will be in the area of the ground that occupies his garden.

A sports promotions company will this month present a business case to Bristol City Council proposing a series of lock gates and weirs be built further down the Avon Gorge, close to Avonmouth, permanently exposing the river's mud banks so they can hold a series of female wrestling events, to be broadcast on Pay-Per-View.

August

HOROSCOPES *by Rose Green*

 Aquarius *(Jan 21 - Feb 19)*

At times this month it could seem like all you're doing is seeing red, every which way you turn will be the same. But don't worry, it's not going to cause any adverse health problems, because it's not anger you're experiencing, it's being surrounded by lobster-faced sunburned Sunday drinkers around the docks.

 Pisces *(Feb 20 - Mar 20)*

Looking forward nervously to a new challenge this autumn on a media studies degree course at the UWE? Worried about the difficulties of student life? Don't worry, it doesn't all have to be doom and gloom, but you know you could save yourself four years by just starting work at Waterstones now.

 Aries *(Mar 21 - Apr 20)*

You really have been doing your bit to save lives recently. Wherever the blood donation van has turned up in Bristol you have been there, prepared to roll up your sleeve and contribute to help ease the blood shortage. Perhaps now is the right time to slow down – I know it's time off work and a free cup of tea, but seven times in one week is too much for anyone.

 Taurus *(Apr 21 - May 21)*

You may dream this month that you go along to the International Balloon Fiesta at Ashton Court, where you stand back and watch in awe as hundreds of different shaped balloons take to the skies. Beware however that trying to live this dream will only end up with you standing around in the pouring rain at 5am, eating an overpriced double cheeseburger, watching nothing.

 Gemini *(May 22 - Jun 21)*

Summer holidays – remember how when you were a kid they seemed to last forever? Well nothing changes when you become a parent. The only real difference of course is that as an adult you'll probably get thrown out of Debenhams for playing in the lifts, bouncing on the beds and writing swear words on the computers. Spoilsports.

 Cancer *(Jun 22 - Jul 23)*

With the Bristol summer coming to a close, now is the time to dust off that barbecue set for one more cremation. Remember the golden rules. Good things to put on the barbecue: sausages, burgers, chicken legs. Things not to put on the barbecue: antifreeze or petrol, especially if you are partial to your garden shed or your eyebrows.

August

 **Leo** *(Jul 24 - Aug 23)*

Bad luck is connected to water for you throughout all of this month. The stars indicate that this probably means that the water you swallowed when swimming in the docks 'for a laugh' was full of rat's piss, and if you don't get yourself down the BRI fast you'll turn into a big scab.

 Virgo *(Aug 24 - Sep 23)*

Did you enjoy yourself in the woods at Ashton Court last month? I bet you did! We saw what you were up to, you dirty sod. Don't think this astrology lark is all one way you know. We're all powerful us mind, we see all. By the way, did you get your jacket clean?

 Libra *(Sep 24 - Oct 23)*

So your dreams of Bristol Medical School evaporated when you opened your exam results. There was no champagne, no celebrations; in fact everyone, including your family, called you a failure. Well that may well be the case. But don't be downhearted, because you are unique, a true one off. Who else nowadays can fail a GCSE?

August

 ## Scorpio *(Oct 24 – Nov 22)*

You are thinking of travelling to foreign shores. Why bother – the weather has been beautiful and there are some lovely beaches just a short drive from Bristol. Who wants to spend twelve hours on a plane trying to get to your destination when you can make that short drive down the M5? Come to think of it – better dig out that passport.

 ## Sagittarius *(Nov 23 – Dec 21)*

Still waiting for your life to live up to the unrealistic expectations of your youth? Well, like waiting for a bus in this fine city, you've got a long wait ahead. My suggestion? Make some sandwiches, put your head down and get used to it. Something will turn up eventually, and it won't be a bus.

 ## Capricorn *(Dec 22 – Jan 20)*

By the end of this month you will have survived the 6 weeks of terror known as the summer holidays. That's 42 days, over 1000 hours, or over 60,000 minutes. Then you can relax as you pack them off to school for their first day of term. What? An In-Service Day – you've got to be joking!

August

Paul Dirac

b. Aug 8th 1902 – d. Oct 20th 1984

It used to be the case that being a celebrity meant you were famous because you were actually good at something. Today however, the requirement of any skill whatsoever no longer seems important. Which is maybe why, despite his importance in the history of the world, super physicist Paul Dirac remains a name that most people have never heard of.

Born in Bishopston, Dirac's legacy to the world is his breakthrough work in linking theories of quantum mechanics with Einstein's Theory of Relativity. It doesn't sound very exciting on paper, but without his work, which has been described as 'poems of science', we simply wouldn't have mobile phones, computers or any of the electronics we take so much for granted today.

One of his most famous mathematical discoveries was the Dirac Equation, something you would have expected him to already know about given that it was named after him. With more squiggles than a child's drawing, this complex equation predicted the existence of an antiworld - a world identical to our own only made from antimatter. His secondary theory of unclematter however was later disproved.

A famously shy man, Dirac was awarded the Nobel Prize for Physics in 1933 (an award he only reluctantly accepted for fear of the publicity if he didn't), and is just the sort of person you would want on your pub quiz team or as your 'Phone a Friend'. His legacy has not only had a profound influence on the modern world, but also on what drunk people argue about down the pub, after football and politics.

The telly comes to town

August 15th 1952 saw the official opening of the BBC transmitter at Wenvoe, South Wales, broadcasting television to Wales and the West. On the day broadcasts started, the *Evening Post* claimed that as many as one Bristol family in twenty-five now owned a television. Sadly only one family in fifty had electricity.

But television was in its infancy, both the programmes and the technology. Sure, it was a marvel, but after half an hour, most of the viewers were already wondering what else was on. The answer to that was – nothing. Lucky really, because remote controls hadn't even been invented yet so you wouldn't have been able to change the channel anyway.

Despite the fact there was nothing to watch, the picture quality was rubbish, and everyone in the street was always staring through your front window, you were still expected to buy a television licence, which would set you back a whopping £2. To make matters worse TV detector vans were already in use in 1952, so evasion was tough. While the detecting technology was crude, it was effective – somebody looking out for a crowd of people gathered around a front room window.

In today's digital world with millions of channels to choose from, it's hard to grasp quite how dull those early shows must have been. The closest thing you could get to it today would be watching back-to-back repeats of *Soccer Night* with the colour turned down.

August

Up, up and, oh hang on, it's a bit windy

For many Bristolians, their experiences of Europe's largest balloon festival involve them getting up at 4am to drive to Ashton Court to watch balloons not take off because it's too foggy, windy, or wet. Either that, or watching a balloon almost knock their chimney off as it loses altitude over Kingswood.

The Night Glow event is always very popular and generally involves huge crowds of people watching balloons not take off to music they've only heard in TV commercials, followed by traffic chaos as they all head for the same narrow exit to get the kids home before morning.

There are, of course, many ways to get to Ashton Court for the festival. You could arrive by bus, coach, or rail (and then of course bus). You cannot however arrive by balloon. Walking is advised, as long as you don't mind a hike, because ironically the Suspension Bridge they love to promote with the balloons will be closed. Never mind, where else in the world can you watch a giant dog chasing a shopping trolley over an empty bridge?

Now in its thirtieth year, times have changed the festival. Other than the popularity and commercialism, the dawning of digital photography means that it's no longer the one event all film developers dread. No longer do they have to spend weeks on end developing blurred photos of distant balloons which just got in the way of them perving over your holiday snaps. Of course most of them are out of a job now anyway. But hey, that's technology for you.

August

Dear IKB

Do you think you could turn your engineering skills to Bristle roads? A suggested starting point here would be stopping all road traffic calming measures and fill in all the bloody pot holes with the money saved.

A second suggestion would be to get shot of all mini-roundabouts, which every Bristolian knows are crap, halve the number of traffic lights and build some more suspension bridges with the money saved on electric. Oh, and sorry to hear of your affliction, I didn't know you were part French.

Ken

IKB SAYS:

What a mess you have got yourself into. It's like I have always known, railways are the answer – no roundabouts to slow you down, no potholes to knock your hat off, no red lights to worry about – well none that any train drivers bother taking notice of.

I say scrap the traffic calming measures, cover the roads in 7-foot Broad Gauge Railway tracks and convert your Vauxhall SRI into a steam engine. Forget electricity all together, it will never catch on. As for building more Suspension Bridges, count me out. They take too much planning, are too expensive to build, and if you hadn't already noticed I'm dead.

PS: I haven't forgotten your jibe about being part French. Tell me this son, just how big is your hat?

Five GWR Presenters From 2007

Andy Bush
Paris Troy
Pit-stop Paulina
Errmm
Ummmmm

Gone But Not Forgotten

Scrolling messages on the Hippodrome
Redcliffe Flyover
Fairfax House
Black and White Café
Bristol Bulldogs Speedway
Tollgate Car Boot Sale

Places That Could Be People

Brandon Hill
Leigh Woods
Lawrence Hill
Bradley Stoke
Lawrence Weston

August

SEPTEMBER

Learn to walk before you run
(particularly if you want to finish the half marathon by Tuesday)

PREDICTIONS

by Rose Green

A police search will start in September after twelve prisoners walk out of Horfield Prison following the popular Open Doors Day organised by the city council. It will be discovered that a newly recruited prison officer misunderstood an _Evening Post_ article detailing the event, and assumed that doors were to be left open on all publicly-owned buildings.

On the anniversary of the launch of BBC Radio Bristol, station bosses will call a crisis meeting after discovering the average age of their audience is now higher than the average person's life expectancy in the UK. However, an overhaul of the playlist fails to materialise once it's discovered that records by pop bands such as the _Arctic Monkeys_ are not available on 78.

A runner who completes the Bristol Half-Marathon dressed as the invisible man will attempt to take legal action against Bristol City Council this month after he fails to appear in the official race results. After much scrutiny of results and interviews with eyewitnesses, it will be found that the real reason he doesn't appear in the results is because he didn't finish until Tuesday.

After losing a lengthy custody battle, a father of seven from Shirehampton will force the Clifton Suspension Bridge to close after he scales one of the towers dressed as Batman, in protest over access to his children. However, despite garnering sympathy from fathers across the city (except those waiting to drive across the bridge), a High Court judge rules that he must still see them.

September

Aquarius *(Jan 21 - Feb 19)*

Do you remember what your Scout leader used to say to you? No, not the stuff about sharing his shorts – I was thinking more about the motto 'be prepared'. Well, perhaps preparation might have been a good thing before entering the Bristol Half Marathon. Never mind, too late to worry now. Remember, if you make the finish it's only half a mile to the BRI.

 Pisces *(Feb 20 - Mar 20)*

Events that are already in motion will become increasingly hard to stop as they start to move at an ever-faster pace. What started out as a bit of fun now doesn't seem so hilarious does it? It's downhill all the way from here I'm afraid – Redcatch Hill that is, in an Escort with no brakes.

 Aries *(Mar 21 - Apr 20)*

While a promotion opportunity may present itself to you this month, it will be best to forget it. Like the proverbial turd in the Feeder, it will be easier for you to float around in the stream of under-achievement than get out of your depth and end up drowning in the fast-flowing river of success.

September

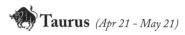

Taurus *(Apr 21 - May 21)*

The last festival of the year in Bristol gives you a final chance to drink yourself stupid, take drugs, roll around in the mud and throw piss-filled bottles at people. Mind you, I get the distinct feeling that with this sort of behaviour it will be the last Kite Festival you will ever be invited to.

Gemini *(May 22 - Jun 21)*

An unpleasant surprise has prompted you to start looking for reasons behind an annoying financial problem. Perhaps you should have acted when told that your endowment policy was under-performing. Now, twenty years on, instead of having enough money to pay of the mortgage on your Bradley Stoke semi, you can't even afford some gnomes for the front garden.

Cancer *(Jun 22 - Jul 23)*

This month it would pay for you to remember the old adage: don't bite off more than you can chew. Not because you're going to get out of your depth in a complicated situation, but mostly because you don't chew your food properly and you'll probably choke.

September

 ## Leo *(Jul 24 - Aug 23)*

You really are a miserable git. Someone thought they once saw you smile but it turned out to be wind. Well they say that laughter is the best medicine; so I prescribe you popping along to Jongleurs in Baldwin Street. The thought of watching comedy should put a smile on your face, though whether it stays there after you've seen the admission price remains to be seen.

 ## Virgo *(Aug 24 - Sep 23)*

The fact that you spent most of last month wandering around Old Market actually looking for an historic Bristolian market highlights the fact that you're probably not that bright and you should probably stay in more this month. Still, at least you know what all those lovely rainbow flags mean now.

 ## Libra *(Sep 24 - Oct 23)*

Following a great night on the town, your friends finally get to see the real you as you decide to reveal your inner self. They may be amused by this sudden, unexpected outpouring, but the taxi driver will be less than happy as you vomit 12 pints of Blackthorn and a Miss Millie's Mega Meal into the back of his taxi.

September

HOROSCOPES
by Rose Green

 Scorpio *(Oct 24 - Nov 22)*

Fortune favours the brave this month – so why not set out on a new and challenging career. Perhaps you could become a security expert in Iraq; a land-mine clearer in Afghanistan; or even a guard on the night bus to Hartcliffe. Perhaps forget the last one, that's just being reckless.

 Sagittarius *(Nov 23 - Dec 21)*

Speed cameras, congestion charging, traffic jams and even policemen disguised as bushes trying to catch you speeding. Commuting around Bristol is certainly no fun. Never mind, all this worry in your life could soon be over as the council has kept their promise to ease traffic congestion; yep, they are re-opening the Clifton Rocks Railway. Now won't that make life easier?

 Capricorn *(Dec 22 - Jan 20)*

Your hair may be turning grey and your body may have seen better days, but that's no reason to start behaving like an old man. Remember the old adage 'it's all in the mind'. So if you want to remain young, discard that cardigan, throw away the Wurthers Originals and make sure you never listen to Radio Bristol after 6 o'clock in the evening.

September

Russ Conway

b. Sep 2ⁿᵈ 1925 – d. Nov 16ᵗʰ 2000

Born Trevor Herbert Stanford, Conway was an ivory tickler of immense skill despite losing a finger in a tragic bread-slicing accident, the likes of which was not seen again in Bristol until they started filming *Casualty*.

From learning to play the organ by sneaking into St Mary Redcliffe Church as a boy, he went on to become one of the nation's most succesful artists of his era, selling over 30 million records. The peak of his recording career came in 1959 when he had five top ten records, two of them number one hits.

Television success followed, with his trademark smile making him a natural for the small screen. Later in life, as music tastes changed, he became renowned as a true granny charmer and his seemingly constant pearly smile even caught the eye of the Queen Mother – although luckily this caused no lasting damage to her sight.

Conway never forgot Bristol, and following successful treatment for stomach cancer in 1989 he set up the Russ Conway Cancer Fund to help fund various good causes. On his 65th birthday in 1990, the first of a long series of charity galas was held at the Bristol Hippodrome, where he played to a full house.

After ten years fundraising, Conway finally succumbed to a recurrence of stomach cancer, which had also by then spread to his brain. His funeral was held on December 6th 2000 at St Mary Redcliffe Church, the birthplace of his keyboard skills.

Nipper

b. c1884 – d. Sep 1895

Forget Lassie, Snoopy, or even Scooby Doo, Nipper is quite possibly the most famous dog of all time. Born in Bristol in 1884, he was named Nipper partly because of his tendency to bite the backs of people's legs and partly because his claws resembled those of a crab.

He was originally owned by Mark Barraud, but following his death (probably from bites to the backs of his legs) he became the property of his brother, the painter Francis Barraud.

It was Francis who painted the now infamous image, *His Master's Voice*, of Nipper looking inquisitively into a gramophone (probably just as he was wondering whether to eat it or cock his leg on it). The Gramophone Company purchased the painting in 1899 and later registered it as a trademark, which they famously used for the record label and store chain, HMV.

Over the years Nipper has appeared on hundreds of millions of records (on the sleeve, not as backing vocals). As well as still being used as the company logo today, Nipper's legacy lives on in Bristol – both as a blue plaque on the house in Clifton in which he was born, and local folklore which has it that you can still hear his bark echo through the HMV store in Broadmead during a full moon.

September

Tying up the loose ends

September 30th 1979 saw the arrival on British television of one of the most unconventional detective shows ever. It was the age of the maverick cop, with uber-cool American cop shows such as *Starsky and Hutch*, *The Streets of San Francisco*, and *Charlie's Angels*. We got *Shoestring*.

Eddie Shoestring was a former computer expert who'd had a nervous breakdown and smashed up a £500,000 computer before becoming a radio phone-in detective who ran around Bristol in a clapped out Ford Cortina estate solving the problems of his listeners. It doesn't sound like the formula for a hit, but hey this was the seventies. It was this or *Mind Your Language*.

With his trademark moustache, 'private ear' Shoestring, portrayed superbly by Trevor Eve, was the mop top cop jock of Bristol town. It was a kind of jovial alternative to *The Sweeny*. Nominated for three BAFTAs, the show ran for just two short series during which Eddie solved murder, poisoning, missing people, kidnapping, domestic abuse, and even hooky imported toys. All of which begs the question: what exactly were police in Bristol doing during the late seventies?

The fictional radio station Shoestring worked for was called Radio West and was set on Welsh Back. A year after the last episode was broadcast the real Radio West opened around the corner in the Watershed. Life imitating art, but was it a fluke or just simply cashing in on free publicity? You decide.

September

Watch that drill mind love…

First broadcast on BBC1 on September 6th 1986, Britain's answer to *ER* has filled our prime-time Saturday viewing schedules with West Country accents so broad they'd only normally be heard on *An Audience with the Wurzels*.

Rewiring a toaster while the washing machine is leaking, working under a car with a hooky looking jack, or just sharpening a knife on the back of your leg, you're either hugely optimistic, plain stupid, or a supporting actor in *Casualty*. The accidents can be seen coming a mile off. "You sure you should be putting all that petrol on that barbecue love?" Not since the Cuprinol man last graced our screens have we enjoyed such wooden acting.

The real heroes are the production team, who painstakingly set up the stunts, and there have been plenty of them over the years, including train crashes, bombings, and fires. All of which makes Holby one of the unluckiest places to live in fictional Britain today. It has even spawned another show in the form of *Holby City,* which itself has given birth to *Holby Blue*. It's becoming a bit like *Gremlins*. At this rate we could soon have a complete channel dedicated to the programme.

The best part of the programme, of course, still remains catching glimpses of the various parts of Bristol you recognise and how they got there. Just how can that ambulance be travelling down Park Street, turn left and end up in Brislington? If only the rest of us in Bristol could get hold of the *A-to-Z* they are using, we could save hours spent stuck in rush hour traffic.

September

Bristol Half Marathon

The biggest annual road running event in Bristol's calendar returns for another year of people slogging up and then back down the Portway wondering exactly how they got roped into it. So if you happen to be running the race this year, here are a few handy tips to help you survive.

Before the start of the race, rub Vaseline into all areas of your body that might chafe. Do not believe anyone who approaches you and claims they are the official Vaseline applier for the half marathon.

Remember to secure your running number firmly to your vest – no number, no medal. Safety pins are best, as using Sellotape will probably see your number vanish into the distance at the first gust of wind. Staples are not advisable.

The runners at the front of the start are probably professionals. So it is probably not a good idea to try to keep pace with them, especially if you are wearing a gorilla suit and diving boots.

When the going gets tough and you really feel like chucking it all in, just remember that all important reason why you are doing it – because you got drunk and said you would. And if that's not a good enough reason, then remember your car is parked near the start.

September

Dear IKB

As an attractive woman in her 'thirties' who has always taken care to look after her body, my life has recently been thrown into turmoil following the announcement from my husband that I was getting fat. Even though I am only a size four, I've been forced to take out insurance to cover my husband's beer, cigarette, and gambling costs should I "balloon into a lardass" and be unable to maintain employment. To capitalise on my misery I have had to take on a third job, to cover the premiums. How can I satisfy my husband and not have to work my fingers to the bone?

Michelle, St Anne's

IKB SAYS:

Reading between the lines of your letter it seems to me that you want to have your cake and eat it too: you want to please your husband and yet you don't want to work? I simply cannot fathom the logic behind such wanton recklessness.

Good God above woman! After I'd spent eighteen hours a day shouting at navvies making sure they were digging my tunnels correctly, the last thing I needed was to come home to a wife who couldn't provide the homely comforts a working man required, and at a time of his choosing.

Let me tell you something, this wonderful industrious nation wasn't built without the sacrifices of the few, and your work-shy sentiment is highly unpatriotic. Next you'll be telling me you want to vote.

September

Things That Just Aren't True

The Shadow Factory used to produce Hank Marvin Records
Clark's Pies are all actually made by a man called Clark
Bristol Blue Glass is given its pigment through excessive swearing

TV Shows Filmed In Bristol

Animal Magic *(1962-84)*
Softly Softly *(1966-69)*
Shoestring *(1979-81)*
The Young Ones *(1982-84)*
Robin of Sherwood *(1984-86)*
Casualty *(1986-)*
Only Fools and Horses *(1988-2003)*
Teachers *(2001-04)*
Deal Or No Deal *(2005-)*
Skins *(2007)*

Streets Named After Badgers

Badger Close *(Longwell Green)*
Badger Sett *(St George)*
Badgers Walk *(Brislington)*
Badgers Holt *(Hengrove)*

September

OCTOBER

Don't put all your plasticine in one warehouse

PREDICTIONS *by Rose Green*

The start of the month will see Bristol University students arriving in the city complete with student loans in hand. Swanky bars and restaurants up and down Whiteladies Road will be packed to bursting point as they spend their nights quaffing bubbly and scoffing caviar until the early hours, followed by a restful snooze, only to be awoken by the alarm of the *Countdown* clock.

Commuters' hopes will be raised once again with talk of another light rail scheme. This one however will not just be light on details, but also track – that is, it will only have one – a monorail. The system, formerly installed at Butlins in Minehead, will be erected around the City Centre, however, due to a lack of salvaged track the only route available will be a loop of the fountains.

Despite surviving the Blitz, decimalisation, and even displaying a 'No thanks to Hallowe'en' poster from the *Evening Post*, pensioners across Bristol will be affronted by a new menace this month. Forget the sweets and fruit, this year trick-or-treat gangs will be armed with the latest in chip and pin technology: "Mastercard or Visa only gran – or the dog gets a banger up his ass".

Towards the end of the month Lidl in Southmead will be awash with unwashed students looking to buy eleven months supply of pasta for 78p on a debit card. Much like their funding, their party lifestyle will already be a distant memory, as the reality of not working for a living hits home. Roll on the Christmas holidays – it's the next chance they'll get for a decent meal.

October

Aquarius *(Jan 21 - Feb 19)*

Can't land that dream job you've been looking for? Do you feel the people around you are holding you back? Well maybe now is the time to drag yourself off the steps of the DSS offices in Fishponds, put your White Lightning cider bottle in the bin, and go out and get a job. Either that, or treat yourself to another bottle of cider.

Pisces *(Feb 20 - Mar 20)*

You have always been a bit of a hoarder, claiming everything will prove useful one day. Well it seems this month you will be right. With the arrival of Hallowe'en you will finally be able to find a use for that box of Terry's All Gold left over from Christmas 1977. At least then the bloody scroungers won't be back again next year.

Aries *(Mar 21 - Apr 20)*

You are envious of all your friends. But try to remember that the grass is always greener on the other side. They may have highly-paid jobs, bigger houses and better cars. But does that make them more successful than you. Well yes, actually it does. But look on the bright side – you are still ahead of the guy who sleeps in the doorway of Debenhams – just.

October

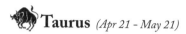 **Taurus** *(Apr 21 - May 21)*

Love matters will come to the fore this month as your fetish for women in masks will be fulfilled when you bump into a group of repulsive witches at a Hallowe'en party in the Horn and Trumpet. Unfortunately, it is not until after you fall under their spell you realise they're not wearing masks - they're just munters.

 Gemini *(May 22 - Jun 21)*

Pack up your troubles in your old kit bag and sod off to Thailand for the winter. What better way to spend your time than working in a bar all-night and partying all day? On your return you will have a great tan to show your friends, the prospect of a new job, and a whole host of appointments at a special clinic in the BRI.

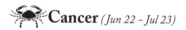 **Cancer** *(Jun 22 - Jul 23)*

Have you recently been feeling like nobody listens to a single word you say? Do you feel like you're constantly being ignored? Does your life feel totally pointless? Well unfortunately that's all part of being a presenter on *Original 106.5 FM*. Don't worry, you'll soon get used to it.

October

HOROSCOPES *by Rose Green*

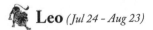 **Leo** *(Jul 24 - Aug 23)*

Fed up of working in a central Bristol call centre? 295 calls waiting – and seven hours until your next thirty second tea break. This month it's time to break free. Throw down your headset; stand on your chair and shout "We're all bloody sheep, can't you see we are all just bloody sheep". Bear in mind though, physical freedom can sometimes be at the expense of financial security.

 Virgo *(Aug 24 - Sep 23)*

Teamwork – that's the buzzword in the Bristol business world. Make sure everyone is working towards the same goal – everyone should be encouraged to make suggestions, irrespective of their grade. Then all you have to do is collect up all the best ideas and pass them off as your own. That's the beauty of being the boss and a tosser to boot.

 Libra *(Sep 24 - Oct 23)*

People are complaining that your spending is getting out of control. Sure, you may be getting yourself heavily into debt trying to keep up with your neighbours, but look on the bright side – when it comes to re-possession time, the telly that comes out of your house in the bailiff's arms will be the widest in the street.

October

 ## Scorpio *(Oct 24 – Nov 22)*

Getting a new job recently filled you with happiness, but now you're in the post you're less cheerful. Sometimes it seems everybody hates you and this feeling of uncertainty is causing you distress. Well don't worry, it's not your imagination, everyone does hate you. That's what happens if you tow people's cars away.

 ## Sagittarius *(Nov 23 – Dec 21)*

Hard up of Henbury – this month could be an important one for you. The planets are in a position that affords you the opportunity of great wealth. Seek out all possibilities for sound financial investment, whether it's on the stock market – through a bank or building society – or just from a random Nigerian email, promising a share of a fortune in return for your bank details.

 ## Capricorn *(Dec 22 – Jan 20)*

It's great to be taken out every once in a while and spoilt rotten. And a man in your position with contracts to award is bound to be popular. Speaking from a business perspective though, it's probably not a good idea to sign legally binding contracts after you have spent the afternoon drinking slammers in the Knights Templar.

October

William 'Fatty' Wedlock

b. Oct 28th 1880 – d. Jan 25th 1965

Affectionately known as 'Fatty' – a nickname today reserved for opposition goalkeepers, referees, and members of Her Majesty's Constabulary – the short and stout Wedlock is still considered one of Bristol City's greatest ever players, racking up an impressive 421 appearances for the club.

As well as captaining the side, Wedlock was capped for England twenty-six times, a feat unlikely to ever be repeated by any Bristol City player, unless a Russian billionaire takes over the club or the national side are struck down by the black death. The Wedlock name still features at Ashton Gate, with the old East End stand being re-named in his honour.

Whereas today's footballers have amassed a fortune before they are old enough to shave, in the good old days, no matter how famous a footballer you were, once you retired from the game you had to venture out into the real world and get a proper job. After retiring from football in 1921, Wedlock didn't have far to travel to his next job – he spent forty-five years running The Star, a pub directly opposite the ground.

In 1981, the pub was re-named The Wedlock's, in honour of the former landlord and player and became a favourite pre- and post-match watering hole for generations of Bristol City fans until its sudden closure in 2005. Unsentimental developers, submitted plans to demolish the pub and replace it with luxury apartments, a plan that has been met with fierce local opposition, not least from Bill's grandson, Fred Wedlock, the oldest protester in town.

October

W G Grace

b. Jul 18th 1848 – d. Oct 23rd 1915

As sporting superstars go William Gilbert Grace was the Victorian equivalent of David Beckham – only minus the tattoos, the ridiculous haircuts, and, of course, he played cricket. Also Beckham isn't 6ft 2in and doesn't sport a beard that would put *ZZ Top* to shame. Oh, and he's not a practising doctor either.

Grace had a surgery in Easton, which is where he spent most of his medical career playing cricket for Gloucestershire and England. Whereas nowadays so-called sportsmen don't even have to time turn up for a drugs test, old WG would've whipped out an appendix before lunch, washed his hands, and then stepped up to the crease to whack out an easy century.

In total, he scored more than 54,000 runs and took an incredible 2,800 wickets. In 1871 alone, he notched up an impressive 2,739 runs along with the worst waiting list in the history of medicine.

Although very athletic and a good runner in his early career, in his later years he became a rather portly figure. Whereas today's cricketers enjoy a diet of pasta and Lucozade Sport, WG preferred half a dozen pork pies and a couple of large whiskeys – and that was just in the tea interval. Not surprisingly, he was often out shortly afterwards.

WG carried on playing until he was 68, after which he enjoyed a short retirement before he died aged 69. Nearly a century on from his death, his beard remains one of the most recognisable in the whole of sporting history.

October

Up in smoke

On Monday October 10th 2005, a major fire ripped through the Aardman Animations storage warehouse close to Temple Meads, taking with it over thirty years of television, film and animation history. The fire raged for three days, destroying virtually everything Aardman had ever produced, including sets, scripts, storyboards and even the Lurpack man, who could sadly only be identified by the initials on his trombone.

From the early days of the simple characters shown on *Vision On*, such as Morph, Chas, and Tony Hart, Aardman moved through the lovable *Creature Comfort* adverts, onto the Oscar-winning escapades of Wallace and Gromit. Over the years, the awards have just kept rolling in, and for Aardman it has been a non-stop success story (apart from *Flushed Away*, but hey, that's what happens when the Americans start getting involved).

It was first thought that the warehouse fire may have been started deliberately and arson was not ruled out. Avon and Somerset Police drew up a list of suspects that included a penguin with a rubber glove on its head, a robotic dog, and a giant rabbit carrying a can of petrol. Fire investigators eventually discovered that the blaze was caused by an electrical fault, ruling out the first ever animated appeal on *Crimewatch* (cracking reconstruction, Gromit).

In the end, for all of Wallace's inventive genius, which has included electronic trousers, various rockets and a bully-proof vest, it was a simple sprinkler system that could have saved much of the history of Aardman.

October

The opening of Cabot Circus

After seemingly eons of disruption in Broadmead and wrangling over the new name, the latest temple of shopping will finally be opened to the credit card-carrying masses.

Broadmead was developed into the main shopping area in Bristol during the 1950s to replace the Castle shopping area, which had been destroyed during the Blitz. Since then, there have been minor improvements made to the area, such as the building of the Galleries shopping centre. This first major overhaul in nearly 60 years is long overdue. In recent years Broadmead has faced strong competition from out of town retail attractions such as the The Mall at Cribbs Causeway, and the Broadwalk shopping centre in Knowle.

Protected by a huge glass roof, it will provide Bristol's shoppers with the chance to wander around posh shops, swanky bars and expensive restaurants in the warm and dry, before popping outside into the cold and buying some cheap shirts and pants in Primark and heading back home with a foot-long tuna toll from Greggs.

Things The Planners Might Say About Cabot Circus

"Don't mention slavery. I did once but I think I got away with it."
"See, I told you it would look just like every other shopping centre."
"Great! I've confirmed the Black and White Minstrels for the opening."

Things The Public Might Say About Cabot Circus

"I remember when this was all roads."
"Where's all the animals muh?"
"Coming down Broadmead?"

October

Dear IKB

As a Bristolian living abroad, I was trying to explain to the people of Leicester about Concorde. They really couldn't understand supersonic flight as all they have here are knitting machines and stone crushers. They haven't even got an iron ship or a Suspension Bridge. I would like to give the people of Leicester a gorge in the hope that it will inspire them to greater things. How should I construct it?

Philip, Leicester

IKB SAYS:

Well you can't really blame simple folk for their lack of capacity for understanding and creation. I'm sure knitting machines and stone crushers have a purpose in society, but I'm not sure what. Can't say I ever needed either during my engineering career, but then I'm a man of intelligence. Well I was anyway.

As to your idea of constructing a gorge, I have to admit it is an admirable one, but you must understand a gorge is not something that you really 'construct' as such. Basically it's just a big hole in the ground - an act of nature, rather than an engineering feat. Nothing technical about it at all I'm afraid. I suppose what you could do is attempt to build a tunnel, do it badly, be over-ambitious, and with a bit of luck it'll collapse in on itself – just try to make sure you're not in it at the time.

October

Former Bristol University Students

Matt Lucas
David Walliams
Simon Pegg
Marcus Brigstocke
Derren Brown

Invented In Bristol

Ribena
Lead Shot
Tarmac
Bristolian

Top Five ITV West Programmes

The West Tonight *(Tuesday)*
The West Tonight *(Thursday)*
The West Tonight *(Wednesday)*
The West Tonight *(Monday)*
The West Tonight *(Friday)*
Soccer Night

October

NOVEMBER

Better late than never
First Bus Customer Charter

A cold start to November will catch the city by surprise, but no one more so than BBC weatherman Richard Angwin who predicts a heat wave and spends the day on College Green wearing just Speedos. With heavy snow and black ice, Bristol's public transport system grinds to a halt. However, nobody will notice for several days – especially Angwin who will be admitted to the BRI with hypothermia of the trunk region.

Despite repeated warnings about the safety of illegally imported fireworks, November 5th will see men armed with rockets bought from an empty carpet shop in Bedminster that wouldn't look out of place in North Korea. November 6th will then see the same men trying to work out if their shed is still somewhere south of the river and how they're going to fill the crater in the lawn.

Latching on to the massive interest generated by anything to do with the enigma that is Banksy, one city councillor will try to cash-in and puts forward the idea of a new "Banksy Holiday" this month. With public holidays in short shrift at this end of the year the plan is initially welcomed by the public, right up until it's discovered the day proposed is actually a Saturday.

After announcing that a top international artist will switch on the Christmas illuminations, thousands flock to the Centre expecting Madonna, Bono, or even that bloke who used to be in *Blackadder*. But bottles start to fly as Latvian performance artist Zito Dromski starts his mime interpretation of electricity in front of the bemused crowd. A council official will be heard muttering, "Thank God we've booked Jim Davidson for next year".

November

Aquarius *(Jan 21 - Feb 19)*

Your boss has long said you need a rocket up your ass. Well, if you walk around Banjo Island this month then that's just what you might end up getting. Whilst the local ASBO gang will undoubtedly be respecting the firework code by not throwing fireworks, that won't actually stop them using a snapped-off drainpipe as a rocket launcher. They might not be putting rockets in their pockets, but they'll certainly be aiming for yours.

Pisces *(Feb 20 - Mar 20)*

Love can sometimes be a difficult beast for you to tackle, but this month with the Christmas party season kicking off, lady luck will shine your way. The stars offer you five words that hold the key to your success in love and you should bear these in mind for they may be subtle clues: Saturday; Horn; Trumpet; Alcohol and Unfussy.

Aries *(Mar 21 - Apr 20)*

Life's a little flat at the moment. Perhaps you really should make the effort and try and be a bit more adventurous this month. Look for new challenges that will excite you, like arranging a bungee jump, going shark fishing or even trying to cross Temple Way during lunch hour.

November

Taurus *(Apr 21 - May 21)*

Be warned, an upcoming weekend of clubbing with a new partner might not be all it seems. You're thinking of a couple of rocking nights at Creation, Warehouse, and the Academy. But they're thinking more of a couple of comfy nights with the East Bristol Caravan club parked up at Keynsham rugby ground. Rummy anyone?

Gemini *(May 22 - Jun 21)*

The nights in Bristol are certainly drawing in now. You go off to work in the dark; you arrive home in the dark. And while you are at work your wife is inviting one of your best mates round for a bit of extra physical action in the bedroom. And where are you? Completely in the dark, that's where.

Cancer *(Jun 22 - Jul 23)*

Tired of living in other people's shadows? Then it's time to strike out. You are master of your own destiny. Just get on that M32 and start driving. Who knows where the journey will take you or where you will end up. Just remember to tell your mum what time you will be home for tea.

November

Leo *(Jul 24 - Aug 23)*

Your friends may tell you that you can't do it; your family may tell you that you can't do it; total strangers may even tell you that you can't do it. But you are determined. It's only when the police tell you that you can't do it that you should stop flashing at passers by on the Bristol to Bath cycle track.

 Virgo *(Aug 24 - Sep 23)*

Penny for them – your thoughts that is, not a badly made guy propped up outside Asda in Bedminster. You are very secretive and rarely reveal what you are thinking to the people closest to you. This month, try to let go of those secrets; you will be better off for it. Unless, of course, you are responsible for a string of vicious murders in the area – in which case, you're probably best keeping it to yourself.

 Libra *(Sep 24 - Oct 23)*

Like a scene from the movie *The Sixth Sense* you spend most of your time wandering around telling everyone "I see dead people". This has won you a whole new set of friends who are impressed with your supposed psychic ability. But will they be as impressed when they discover you actually work at the Co-op Funeral Services in Redfield?

November

Scorpio *(Oct 24 - Nov 22)*

Doesn't your house seem empty now that your only child has left home for university? Well that's probably because you have had to sell all your possessions to pay for the first year's tuition fees. Never mind – rest assured that it will all be worth it. Nothing will prepare them better for a job in a call centre than three years at Bristol University.

Sagittarius *(Nov 23 - Dec 21)*

Job stability looks uncertain this month as you run for your early morning bus only to see the back end of it disappearing away down Southmead Road. But don't worry, you will learn from this? If only that it's a bad idea to leave the engine running when you leave it to buy your fags.

Capricorn *(Dec 22 - Jan 20)*

What are the main ingredients for a perfect life? Career, romance, family and wealth. So, you are thinking, what's stopping me combining them all? Surely this would be the formula for unabridged happiness? Well, technically no, as romance with family is against the law in this particular part of the West Country, so leave well alone (or move to the Forest of Dean).

November

Steve Merchant

b. Nov 24th 1974

From humble comedy beginnings in a room above the now defunct *Bristol Flyer*, Merchant – officially the tallest thing ever to rise out of Hanham (with the exception of a rusty green light) – has gone on to become the lesser well-paid half of one of Britain's most successful comedy duos – the All New Little and Large.

Merchant met his comedy collaborator, Ricky Gervais, after applying for a job as his assistant at radio station XFM. It was to be a comedy partnership made in Slough, when the first series of their unique sitcom *The Office* hit the screens and made both of them more successful than they could have ever imagined. First broadcast in 2001, the show went on to win awards all over the world, as well as spawning a host of lucrative adaptations in several countries.

Following on from their first multi award-winning outing, Merchant moved out from behind the camera to portray inept agent Darren Lamb to Gervais' rising star Andy Milman, in the further award winning sitcom *Extras*. In doing so, he also inadvertently took the total number of authentic Bristolian accents on national television to a gurt macky three.

But despite huge international success, the Bristolian beanpole has still to rub shoulders with Hollywood A-list celebrities such as Tom Cruise, Danny DeVito, or even R2-D2. Unfazed by such issues, the Mr Nice Guy of British comedy prefers to shun the limelight for a quiet night in with a nice cup of tea and the Internet.

Edward 'Blackbeard' Teach

b. c1680 – d. Nov 22ⁿᵈ 1718

Probably single-handedly responsible for why pirates sound as if they're all from the West Country, Bristol-born Blackbeard was to honest sea-faring folk what Bernard Matthews is to a turkey – somebody you wouldn't relish seeing coming over the horizon.

Teach started his nautical career as a privateer – basically pirates for hire, employed by someone else to do their dirty work for them. But after work dried up – thanks to too many peace treaties being signed – he turned his hand to robbing people for his own profit in an early form of self-contracting.

Despite having fourteen wives, he wasn't really the kind of chap you'd relish your daughter bringing home. Although dinner with the in-laws could've been quite interesting. With a bandolier stuffed with more weaponry than a brigade of squaddies in Iraq, he rarely found himself short of a sword, knife, or pistol during a fight. But just in case the weapons weren't enough to scare you, his party trick of setting fire to his plaited beard ensured you knew he hadn't come aboard for tea and biscuits.

But the life of a notorious pirate is a short one and in the autumn of 1718, just two years into his career, Teach was caught short by the Royal Navy. Following a couple of days of heavy pirate partying, the navy launched a surprise attack that ended up seeing Blackbeard killed and decapitated. His head was hung from a navy ship to prove that he really was dead, and not, as some legends state, to help them see where they were going.

November

Home James!

Since its first flight in 1969, Bristol's most famous technological marvel has been synonymous with speed, elegance, and big noses in equal measure. Sure it's fast as a bullet from a rifle, yes it's as graceful as swan, but it's also the perfect nickname for anyone with a whopping hooter.

Built by a bunch of very clever people in Filton (and a couple in France) back in the days when hi-tech meant vinyl and valves, Concorde sadly ended up being as magnificent a commercial failure as it was a plane. Passenger services began in 1976 to a handful of destinations, but expansion of these routes was hampered by complaints about noise. Despite the fact that you could now cross the Atlantic so quickly you could arrive before you actually left, it was like your gran farting – nobody wanted to hear it.

In April 2003, both British Airways and Air France announced the retirement of the entire Concorde fleet, and Wednesday November 26th 2003 saw Concorde's final flight. Concorde 216, the last to be built at Filton, performed a farewell flight over of Bristol. She was watched by thousands of people who skived off work to catch a glimpse, before coming in to land at Filton to an emotional crowd, many of whom had helped to build her. There she rusts in peace, on show to a nostalgic public.

After 34 years of flying, and even now in retirement, Concorde remains an aviation icon, a credit to the people of Bristol, and the only supersonic passenger aircraft named after a pub in Stockwood.

November

International Short Film Festival

Billed as the UK's most important short film festival (films of a short duration that is, not a festival that only runs for a couple of hours), it's the place to be if you don't have the attention span to stay awake through *The Lord of The Rings*.

This prestigious festival is Bristol's annual answer to Cannes, only without the glitz and glamour of the French Riviera. They might have a marina full of playboy yachts, magnums of Champagne, and call each other darling, but we've got the *SS Great Britain*, flagons of cider, and call each other me babber. No contest.

Switching on the Christmas Lights

It used to be the case that the switching on of the Christmas illuminations was accompanied by the Bristol Carnival – a chance for people to stand around the Centre in the freezing cold watching other people in tights go past on the back of a lorry whilst pretending to be part of a big cake. No they weren't mental (well not all of them anyway), it was for charity.

Now switching on the Christmas lights is merely a chance for people to stand around the Centre in the freezing cold waiting for somebody who was once a little bit famous to flick a switch. I can't help thinking we're missing something here.

November

Dear IKB

Now that winter has arrived in Bristle, I like to wear a hat to keep my big head warm. Unfortunately, when I take the hat off, my hair looks like I've been electrocuted. As you are a hat wearer of distinction, can you give any tips?

Heidi, Patchway

IKB SAYS:

Wearing a hat is always a good idea as it makes you look taller, which in my case obviously was quite important. But as you have become aware, serious styling issues can arise from covering your head. This was never an issue for me as I rarely took my hat off, and when I did, my thinning barnet never attempted to put up a fight, staying stuck to my head. The goose fat also helped to keep it down.

As a lady, I can assume that you would not be interested in the use of animal fats to keep your hair close to your head, so I have engineered up a solution for you. It is quite simple, and, of course, involves steam.

Basically what you require is a small boiler inside your hat which would emit a slow and steady flow of steam onto your head whenever it is covered. This has two benefits. One it will keep your hair from turning wild upon the removal of your hat, and two it is more environmentally friendly than any hairspray product you can buy. Quite where you keep the coal to fuel the boiler whilst out and about I have yet to finalise.

November

Surviving an Emergency in Bristol

Should an emergency break out, try to salvage that government emergency pamphlet you used to line the bottom of the hamster cage. If you are trying to work out why you would need a large bag of gravel and some fence panels to survive, then you are probably reading the *Wickes* catalogue that came free with the *Bristol Observer*.

In the event of a major disaster, local television stations will broadcast public safety advice. But pay particular attention if you are watching ITV West, as any instructions will be broken up by commercials for HeliBeds, who under the circumstances may not be able to deliver by bedtime.

Although public transport would grind almost certainly to a halt in the event of a terrorist attack on the city, you may not notice for some time – especially if you are sitting at Lawrence Hill waiting for a driver to arrive.

If your house is bombed and you find yourself trapped in rubble with your elderly grandparents, try to humour them as they tell you that it's not anywhere near as bad as the Blitz was; they don't make bombs like they used to; or ask what time is the Queen Mother likely to arrive.

If all power to your property is cut, leaving you with no form of heating and you are in the middle of a cold snap of weather, under no circumstances try to keep warm by wearing your coat indoors. Whilst this may seem like a good idea, you will not feel the benefit of it when you do eventually go out.

November

DECEMBER

A good man is hard to find
(especially on the dance floor of Chicago Rock Café)

Pantomime will make a welcome return to the Bristol Hippodrome this month, following a break of two years with a production of Babes in the Wood. However, initial enthusiasm will disappear after it is announced that the lead role will be played by seventies rock superstar, and former Horfield resident, Gary Glitter.

Following the success of the Bristol edition of Monopoly, a new Bristolian edition of the 'I know much longer and more cleverer words than you' game of Scrabble will hit the shops in time for the Christmas rush. Whilst most of the rules will remain the same, the letter bag will contain thirty more Ls than the original.

Environmentalists across the world will this month celebrate massive savings in global energy usage after successfully persuading businesses across the world to reduce power consumption and consider their carbon footprint. However, all planetary gains will unfortunately be wiped out in a single night as Smith's Auto Services in St George switch on their annual festive illuminations.

Kingswood retailers will be forced to close after a local man installs an ice rink at the Kings Chase precinct. Inspired by the open-air rink at Cribbs Causeway, the man will flood the pavement on a cold night to create his own Christmas cash cow. A police spokesman will announce he is "skating on thin ice" and is on "a slippery slope", heading towards spending Christmas at Her Majesty's pleasure.

December

Aquarius *(Jan 21 - Feb 19)*

The kids wanted a dog for Christmas, but there is no way any responsible person in Bristol will sell you one so close to Christmas. So instead of letting down the children, you have stolen one. Just imagine their joy when they receive it. Let's just hope the RSPCA didn't have any security cameras.

 Pisces *(Feb 20 - Mar 20)*

You have worked really hard this year, impressing people along the way with your dedication and attention to detail. You could be in line for that long overdue promotion. So now is the time to blow it all by drinking a jug of Bacardi Breezer at the works party and smacking your boss in the mouth. It is Christmas after all.

 Aries *(Mar 21 - Apr 20)*

Who needs the stress of Christmas? Packed shops, no parking, and drunken office workers on the rampage. Why not pop along to Bristol International Airport and book a flight to the sunshine. Imagine spending Christmas day relaxing on the beach, enjoying a cocktail. Just don't forget to ring the wife and kids to wish them a Happy Christmas.

December

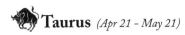 **Taurus** *(Apr 21 - May 21)*

Short of cash over the festive season? Why not use your entrepreneurial spirit to get you out of a hole. Get yourself down to Frenchay Forestry, buy a shed-load of Christmas trees, find an empty shop and bang them out at twice what you paid for them. It seems to work for everybody else.

 **Gemini** *(May 22 - Jun 21)*

This month you will start to get that Christmas feeling when your idiot neighbour decides to put his giant plastic Santa onto his roof. But it's not really Christmas – not until your mum starts moaning about how it doesn't seem like Christmas, every car park in Broadmead is full to over-flowing, and you end up getting assaulted on Park Row by some gorilla wearing a Christmas hat.

Cancer *(Jun 22 - Jul 23)*

Accidents will happen – just like the time you fell out of the tree while spying on your neighbour in the shower. But remember – most accidents are preventable – even more so if you stop driving your bus around Bristol city centre at 60 miles an hour while trying to read a copy of the Sun.

December

Leo *(Jul 24 - Aug 23)*

There's an old saying, "You are beginning to get old when all your friends start appearing in the Deaths section of the *Evening Post*". Well fear not – there's still life in the old dog yet. Just as long as this month you manage to avoid paper-reading bus drivers in the city centre and large plastic Santas falling from Bristol rooftops.

 Virgo *(Aug 24 - Sep 23)*

Are the darker nights and cold weather getting you down? What you need this month is to get out and enjoy yourself. What better way than a good seasonal pantomime? I know recent years have seen a dearth of panto in Bristol, but at least this year Jim Davidson's still nowhere to be seen. Proof if needed that there is a God.

 Libra *(Sep 24 - Oct 23)*

Christmas is coming and the goose is getting fat, please put a penny in the old man's hat. Well, when I say hat, I mean the cardboard bottom of a case of beer. Allowing your charitable inner self to help Broadmead's beggars this month could in turn help you, especially if you're a crack dealer.

December

Scorpio *(Oct 24 - Nov 22)*

You are an accident waiting to happen this month. Don't re-wire anything, don't try to cross the centre, don't try to find adventure in city centre nightclubs, don't try walking to the shops on a plastic hip, and whatever you do, don't attempt to get your decorations out of the loft. Hello? Hello? Are you still there?

 # Sagittarius *(Nov 23 - Dec 21)*

You are unhappy about your appearance and have been considering some form of cosmetic surgery. This can be very expensive and the results are not guaranteed. Why not instead spend your Saturday evening drinking in Kingswood – where, chances are, someone will rearrange your face free of charge.

 # Capricorn *(Dec 22 - Jan 20)*

The moons of Jupiter, the rings of Saturn and the Christmas lights from the Mall in Cribbs Causeway are all entering your astrological plane, feeding power and strength into the deepest crevices of your soul. Avoid broccoli and men named Kenneth.

December

Sara Dallin
b. Dec 17th 1961

Although her name may not be instantly recognisable, *Bananarama*, the band she helped to form, certainly is. Sara (the better-looking blond one of the three) met fellow Bristolian and future band mate Karen Woodward growing up in Downend. She later went to study at the London College of Fashion (a bit of a surprise given how the band used to dress) where she met Siobhan Fahey, and in 1981 the three girls formed *Bananarama*.

The band was given its first big break when former *Specials* front man Terry Hall asked them to perform with his new band the *Fun Boy Three*. A string of hits followed, including *Cruel Summer*, *Robert De Niro's Waiting* and the football terrace favourite *Na Na, Hey Hey, Goodbye*.

In 1983 the girls became part of music history when they were one of only two female acts invited to appear on the *Band Aid* single *Do they know this will get played every bloody Christmas*. When the record was re-recorded in 1989, they became the only band to appear on both versions.

Whereas artists today can get a top 10 hit by getting their mum to buy a CD, the girls sold over 40 million records and had global success. Never manufactured or choreographed – one look at their dancing proved this – they continued to knock out the hits long after their peers had disappeared. Still recording and touring as a duo (just the Bristol lasses remain), you can forget the *Spice Girls*, *Sugababes* and *Girls Aloud* – the original girl power was two-thirds Bristolian.

Bridging the gap

The idea of a bridge over the Avon Gorge was originally conceived by wealthy Bristol merchant, William Vick, who in 1754 left £1000 in his will to be invested until it became £10,000, when it was to be used to build a bridge. While in the 18th century £10,000 might have seemed ample funding, particularly to a man who knew nothing about bridges, by the time the project came to life, it wasn't even enough to cover a round of bacon sandwiches for the navvies.

In 1829, a competition was launched to find the best design. Promoted as *Bridge Idol*, the queue for contenders stretched around the block from the Marriot Hotel. One at a time, designers went before the panel of judges headed up by Thomas Telford, himself an engineering mogul, only to be dismissed. In the end, Telford decided that everyone else's ideas were crap and that he would award himself the commission. Unsurprisingly this wasn't a very popular decision and a second competition, *Bridge Academy*, was launched, won by a young Isambard Kingdom Brunel.

Work started in 1831, but development was continually fraught with problems, including shortfalls in finance and rioting. Ironically, it was the death of Brunel that would give the project the kick-start it needed to reach completion. The iconic (if somewhat over-used) symbol of Bristol officially opened to the public on December 8th 1864. Today, the bridge carries around 12,000 vehicles each day (or none if the Ashton Court Festival or the Balloon Fiesta are on).

December

Seeing in the New Year

"Should old acquaintance be forgot and… mumble, mumble, and mumble". Yes, you've waited a full twelve months for the return of the biggest anti-climax of the year. So, if you haven't drunk enough over the last week, then it's best to hit the streets and celebrate.

For many this means heading for the city centre, where bars that were free yesterday (and will be tomorrow) cost £40 to get in, booze is flowing like it's going out of fashion, and any municipal fountain becomes a magnet for standing in. Following this, there's the joy of spending hours trying to get a taxi home for a small fortune (where's the Hofmeister bus when you need it?)

Alternatively there is always a party at a neighbour's house where the only booze on offer will be Skol lager or a bottle of Advocat. At midnight you will be forced to pile outside into a freezing cold street so you can stand around awkwardly watching a load of other strangers standing around awkwardly. The banging of saucepans begins – unless, of course, you live in Bishopston, as the Le Creuset frying pan is too heavy to lift (and too expensive to play with).

Despite hundreds of fireworks going off in the sky, there will still be one person sat inside the house refusing to come outside as their watch says it's still one minute to twelve. Sound depressing? That's because it usually is. And the most depressing thing of all is you will be back to work in just over a day's time. Happy 2009!

December

Dear IKB

I need your engineering expertise to overcome a serious problem. I have just bought a six-foot tall artificial Christmas tree from Aldi but the base is so wobbly the bloody thing won't stand up for more than thirty seconds. How can I prevent it from constantly collapsing and ultimately ending up in our Christmas dinner?

Brian, Henbury

IKB SAYS:

Luckily, you have come to the right man. Many of my structures were put up nearly two hundred years ago and have stood the test of time - all apart from that bit at Temple Meads by the car park but that's down to a botched patch job done back in the 60s.

Your toppling tree is a simple problem to solve. Firstly, you need to anchor the tree. I would suggest using steel chains burrowed into the ground to a depth of around thirty metres. Then you will need to construct two giant towers either side of the tree, each to the height of around eight-six feet. From there you can build a simple one hundred and sixty-two rod suspension system to support the tree. Alternatively, you could always purchase a new tree – whichever seems easier.

December

Items Made From Bristol Blue Glass

Cufflinks *(£25)*
Small Tall Jug *(£26)*
Penguin *(£48)*
Ship's Decanter *(£95)*
Prices correct at time of print

Nightclubs Your Parents Might Have Met In

The Glen *(Redland Hill)*
Locarno *(Frogmore Street)*
Romeo & Juliet's *(Nelson Street)*
Parkside *(Bath Road)*
Chasers *(Regent Street)*
Town's Talk *(Bridgewater Road)*
Millionaires Club *(Stapleton Road)*
The Granary *(Welsh Back)*

Not To Be Put In Your Brown Recycling Box

Glass
Metal
Children
Nuclear Waste

December

Do you need help?

He's built bridges, boats, railways, and tunnels, and
he's even tackled death, but now, through the power
of Bristolian medium Rose Green, Isambard
Kingdom Brunel, Bristol's only adopted half-French
Victorian short-ass genius is here to solve your
problems and dilemmas.

So if your life in such a mess that you desperately
need help from a dead fanatical steam enthusiast, why
not visit www.thatbebristle.co.uk and tell us all. We'll
channel your problems through Rose, and the most
entertaining problems (and answers) will be credited
and included in the next *Old Bristle Almanac*.

My favourite Bristolians

NOTES

I would like to ask IKB...

NOTES

What really happened this year

Crap Evening Post headlines

NOTES

Records played by BBC Radio Bristol

NOTES

Some buses I caught in 2007